Self-Help
STUFF THAT
WORKS

Self-Help

STUFF THAT

WORKS

Adam Khan

YOUME WORKS

BELLEVUE WASHINGTON

Published by
YouMe Works
PO Box 1703
Bellevue WA 98009

Contact the author or publisher
online at www.YouMeWorks.com

ISBN   0-9624656-7-4

Library of Congress Card Number: 98-88998

Manufactured in the United States

Editor, Consultant, and Confidante: J. Klassy Evans
Copy Editor: Vicki McCown
Cover Design: Bill Fletcher
Photo credit: J. Klassy Evans

FIRST EDITION

Contents

Part Two: Work

Part Three: People

Self-Help
STUFF THAT
WORKS

Introduction

IF I WERE SITTING DOWN TO READ this book for the first time, my question would be: "What will I gain by reading this book?"

The answer is: You will gain a large number of ideas you can *apply*—practical ideas that will help you make your circumstances better. And you will get those ideas separately: Each chapter is independent from the others and can be read in any order. And the ideas are served up in bite-size, easily digestible chunks.

This book covers a broad spectrum of feelings and situations, so at any given time and for any given circumstance, you could profitably look in here and find something useful—some principle you could apply that would improve your situation or your attitude toward it.

The main thing you'll get from this book is a collection of methods you can use to direct your actions more effectively. For example, if you try to vent when you're angry so you don't "hold it inside," you'll find out on page 250 that venting doesn't work—and why. And you'll find out what *does* work. The ideas in this book will help you direct your actions so that the things you want to happen will be more likely to happen.

Self-Help Stuff That Works is a collection of articles I wrote, mostly for my column *Adam Khan on Positive Living* in the newsletter *At Your Best*, published by Rodale Press. When I decided to compile them into a book, they naturally arranged themselves into three categories: attitude, work, and relationships. There were some odd exceptions—a few articles on how to make changes in general—and I added one or two to each section to help you translate the ideas into real improvement in the quality of your life.

Are you ready? Okay, but we have one more thing to cover: How to get the most out of this book—the subject of the next chapter.

All of us are self-made, but only the successful will admit it.

— Earl Nightingale

How to Use This Book

MOST OF THESE ARTICLES, which are now chapters, are short, but highly condensed. Think of this book as an all-you-can-eat buffet where you pick and choose what you want for now. You can come back again for more at some other time. *It is impossible for you to digest the contents of this book in one reading—there is too much here.* Please reread and remember that sentence. It is important.

Since the chapters are in no particular order, you can browse around the book until you find something that sparks your interest and read that, leaving the rest until later. Even if you read straight through the book, some chapters will strike you as especially relevant—they'll answer a current need or situation in your life. When that happens, copy the principle (stated at the end of each chapter) onto a card and carry the card with you for a few days or weeks or even months, concentrating on putting that principle into practice.

Then come back to the book and find another principle or two to practice for a while. Don't try to practice too many at a time—one or two, maybe three at the most.

Or browse the book before you go to bed each night to find a principle you want to practice the next day. Write the principle on a card, and start practicing it first thing in the morning.

Another good use for the book is to refer to it when you're down. When you feel stressed or frustrated or worried or any negative emotion, leaf through the book looking for a chapter that can help you with that.

As you read, keep a highlighter handy and mark passages that have special meaning for you.

READING THIS BOOK once wouldn't come close to maximizing its value. If you read this book start to finish this week, a year from now you will have forgotten almost all of it. At that time you may be dealing with a troublemaker at work, and even though pages 179-181 give you a good way to handle it, a year from now those ideas are likely to have been buried in a year's worth of new information and memories, stashed somewhere in the back of your mind, unavailable to you.

The things we learn are *not* etched in stone. They are stored in a gooey organ. And you use that organ—your brain—every day. New ideas and experiences pass through your brain all the time, so what you know fades and is less available to your working memory—except the stuff you use repeatedly. That's why I recommend referring to this book when you're down. It makes a difference. I do it myself and I wrote the book! Insights can fade from our awareness. They get crowded out by the urgencies of the day.

Use a principle enough times, and it will become a permanent part of your character. But in the meantime, refer to the book when you need it. And consult it when you want to help your friends. This book was made to be *used*. So let's get to it.

The spirit of self-help is the root of all genuine growth in the individual; and, exhibited in the lives of many, it constitutes the true source of national vigor and strength. Help from without is often enfeebling in its effect, but help from within invariably invigorates.

— Samuel Smiles (excerpted from his book Self-Help, *the first book of its kind, published in 1859)*

Attitude

Optimism

IT'S AN AGE-OLD BATTLE. Pessimists think optimists are foolish, optimists think pessimists make themselves unnecessarily miserable. A lot of research has been done on this issue in the last 30 years. Have we answered the question yet? Is the glass half-full or half-empty?

Martin Seligman and his colleagues at the University of Pennsylvania found that optimistic people are happier than pessimists. When something bad happens, optimists think of it as temporary, limited in its effect, and not entirely their fault. Pessimists do the opposite. They consider the setback to be permanent, far-reaching and *all* their fault. There are varying degrees of this, of course; it's not black or white. Most people fall somewhere between the two extremes.

The main difference between optimists and pessimists is *how they explain setbacks to themselves.* Using these definitions, researchers find that optimism contributes to good health and pessimism contributes to illness. In several large-scale, long-term, carefully controlled experiments, Seligman discovered that optimists are more successful than pessimists—optimistic politicians win more elections, optimistic students get better grades, optimistic athletes win more contests, optimistic salespeople make more money.

Why would this be so? Because optimism and pessimism *both* tend to be self-fulfilling prophecies. If you think a setback is permanent, why would you try to change it? Pessimistic explanations tend to make you feel defeated—making you *less* likely to take constructive action. *Optimistic* explanations, on the other hand, make you *more* likely to act. If you think the setback is only temporary, you're apt to try to do something about it, and because you take action, you *make* it temporary. It becomes a self-fulfilling prophecy.

Pessimistic people do have one advantage: They see reality more accurately. It's the attitude to adopt if you're attempting something risky or dangerous. But be careful because one of the biggest counts *against* pessimism is that it causes depression. More accurately, pessimism sets up the condition for depression to occur. One bad setback can knock a pessimist into the pit. Since depression costs this country more per year than heart disease (the nation's number one killer), pessimism has serious side effects. It's kind of a booby-prize for a pessimist to be able to say, "Yes, but I see reality more accurately."

The good news is that a pessimist can learn to be an optimist. Pessimists can learn to see the temporary aspects of setbacks. They can be more specific about the effects of it, they can learn to *not* take all the blame and they can learn to take credit for the good they do. All it takes is practice. Optimism is simply a way of thinking about good and bad; it's a cognitive skill anyone can learn.

So, what about the age-old conflict? Is the glass half-full or half-empty? Our best answer is that the glass is both half-full *and* half-empty, but you're much better off if you think of it as half-full.

When bad happens:
Assume it won't last long, look to see what *isn't* affected, and don't indulge in self-blame.

When good happens:
Consider its effects permanent, see how much of your life is affected, and look to see how much you can take credit for.

Mistakes are only what you make of them.

— *Danielle Stouter*

Optimism is Healthy

CHRIS PETERSON WAS TEACHING a class in abnormal psychology at Virginia Tech when he told his students to fill out an Attributional Style Questionnaire—a carefully designed test that determines a person's level of optimism and pessimism. The students also answered questions about their general health, including how often they went to a doctor.

Peterson followed the health of his students the following year and discovered that the pessimists had twice as many infectious diseases and made twice as many trips to the doctor as the optimists.

Later, Martin Seligman of the University of Pennsylvania and two of his colleagues, using interviews and blood tests, found that optimists have better immune activity than pessimists. Studies by other researchers show the same thing. Why? One big factor is that "Pessimistic individuals," as Seligman writes, "get depressed more easily and more often."

When a person is depressed, certain brain hormones become depleted, creating a chain of biochemical events that end up slowing down the activity of the immune system. For example, two key players in our immune systems are T cells and NK cells.

T cells recognize invaders (like viruses) and make more copies of themselves to kill off the invaders. Pessimists' T cells don't multiply as quickly as optimists', allowing invaders to get the upper hand.

NK cells circulate in the blood and kill whatever they come across that they identify as foreign (like cancer cells). Pessimists' NK cells can identify foreign entities, but they don't destroy them as well as the optimists' NK cells.

OPTIMISTS ALSO LOOK at information in more depth to find out what they can do about the risk factors. In a study by Lisa Aspinwall, PhD, at the University of Maryland, subjects read health-related information on cancer and other topics. She discovered that optimists spent *more* time than pessimists reading the severe risk material and they remembered more of it.

"These are people," says Aspinwall, "who aren't sitting around wishing things were different. They believe in a better outcome, and that whatever measures they take will help them to heal." In other words, instead of having their heads in the clouds, optimistic people look. They do more than look, they seek. They aren't afraid to look into the situation *because* they're optimistic. Thus, for yet another reason, optimists are likely to be healthier.

The best news is what research has shown repeatedly: Anyone can become more optimistic with effort. And every effort you make to keep an optimistic attitude will reward you with a stronger immune system. So you'll enjoy better health. And it is also true that the better your health, the easier it is to maintain an optimistic outlook.

Become more optimistic.

Finding temporary and specific causes
for misfortune is the art of hope:
Temporary causes limit helplessness in time,
and specific causes limit helplessness
to the original situation.

— Martin Seligman

A Wiser Adviser

HAVE YOU EVER NOTICED how wise you are when you give advice to a person younger than you? You aren't fooling yourself. You really have gained some wisdom over the years. Have you ever wished you could be that wise when *you* had troubles? You can. You can talk to *yourself* like a "Dutch uncle."

Randall Masciana, M.S., tried to find out what kind of mental strategy would improve a person's performance when throwing darts. Masciana had the participants try everything from mental imagery to Zen. What worked best for improving the dart thrower's ability to hit the target was "positive self-talk."

Simply talking to yourself in a confident, reassuring, positive, friendly way makes a difference. It may be trite. It may be old. But it works, and it works better than anything else.

When things get tough, *keep your thoughts prominent.* Turn up the volume of your inner voice so you can hear it clearly and coach yourself. If you don't know what to say, imagine a friend of yours or your little brother in the same situation and say to yourself what you would say to them.

Another way of knowing what to say to yourself is to ask yourself what someone you admire would say to you: Abraham Lincoln, a professor, your grandmother— whomever you admire for her or his wisdom and strength of character. Imagine asking the person for advice and imagine what s/he might say to you.

You know more about your own situation than anyone else, so your advice to yourself is in some ways more useful than anyone else's. You *are* wise. If you would only talk to yourself and *listen*, your life would be better.

Talk to yourself in a confident, reassuring, positive way.

Our lives are what our thoughts make them.

— *Marcus Aurelius*

Honest Abe

WE CELEBRATE ABRAHAM LINCOLN'S birthday
(February 12), and we should. Lincoln was one of the
few great men who really was great. Before he became
president, Lincoln spent twenty years as an unsuccessful
Illinois lawyer—at least he was unsuccessful in financial
terms. But when you measure the good he did, he was
very rich indeed. Legends are often untrue, but Lincoln
was the real thing. George Washington never chopped
down a cherry tree, but Abraham Lincoln *was* honest.
During his years as a lawyer, there were hundreds of docu-
mented examples of his honesty and decency.

For example, Lincoln didn't like to charge people
much who were as poor as he was. Once a man sent him

twenty-five dollars, but Lincoln sent him back ten of it, saying he was being too generous.

He was known at times to convince his clients to settle their issue out of court, saving them a lot of money, and earning himself nothing.

An old woman in dire poverty, the widow of a Revolutionary soldier, was charged $200 for getting her $400 pension. Lincoln sued the pension agent and won the case for the old woman. He didn't charge her for his services and, in fact, paid her hotel bill and gave her money to buy a ticket home!

He and his associate once prevented a con man from gaining possession of a tract of land owned by a mentally ill girl. The case took fifteen minutes. Lincoln's associate came to divide up their fee, but Lincoln reprimanded him. His associate argued that the girl's brother had agreed on the fee ahead of time, and he was completely satisfied.

"That may be," said Lincoln, "but I am *not* satisfied. That money comes out of the pocket of a poor, demented girl; and I would rather starve than swindle her in this manner. You return half the money at least, or I'll not take a cent of it as my share."

He was a fool, perhaps, by certain standards. He didn't have much, and it was his own fault. But he was a good human being by anyone's standards and I'm glad we celebrate his birthday.

Honesty makes you feel good about yourself and creates trust in others. It improves your relationship with yourself and with others. It's not much in fashion these days to talk about the benefits of honesty and decency, but the benefits are there and they are valuable and worth the trouble.

Lincoln didn't talk much about religion, even with his best friends, and he didn't belong to any church. But he once confided to a friend that his religious code was the same as an old man he knew in Indiana, who said, "When I do good, I feel good, and when I do bad, I feel bad, and that's my religion."

Honesty. It may be corny, but it's the finest force for good in the world, and it always will be.

Do some honest good in the world.

Honesty is the first chapter in the book of wisdom.

— Thomas Jefferson

Think of people you really admire and emulate the thing that makes them admirable: They're being themselves.

— Mike Elgan

Master the Art of Making Meaning

YOUR MIND IS A MEANING-MAKING MACHINE. Without even trying, you "know" what things mean, at least most of the time. When someone treats you rudely, your mind interprets that. It makes some meaning out of it. And it's completely automatic. That is, you don't stop and think about it. You don't *try* to make an interpretation. It happens without any effort on your part.

The meanings you make affect the way you feel and determine how you interact with people and circumstances. The interpretations you make about the events in your life have a significant influence on the amount of stress you experience in your day.

For example, let's say someone cuts you off on the freeway. And let's further postulate, just for fun, that your automatic interpretation is "What a jerk." The interpretation would probably make you upset, at least a little bit. But realize that it doesn't feel like you're making the *interpretation* "What a jerk." The way it feels to you is that your assessment of the person is obvious, and anyone in their right mind would make the same assessment in the same circumstances. But believe it or not, your interpretation was your own doing, and it wasn't the only possible interpretation you could have made.

The important thing about this is that your interpretations change the way you feel, *and those feelings change the way you interact with the world.*

The good news is: You're not stuck with the interpretations your mind makes automatically. You can come up with new ones. You wouldn't marry the first person you met after puberty, would you? You wouldn't take a job at the first place you saw a "Help Wanted" sign, would you? Well, you don't have to use the first interpretation that pops into your head, either.

In the example above, the possible ways to interpret someone cutting you off are virtually unlimited. How about this one: The person had unexpected car trouble and now is running terribly late to an important appointment. If the driver is a woman, maybe she's in labor and needs to get to a hospital *now*. If it's a man, maybe he was called at work and told his wife is in labor. Maybe his brakes went out. Maybe he's having heart trouble.

None of those interpretations are better than any others in an absolute way. But which one leaves you able to go on about your day feeling fine? Or, if it's a situation that keeps repeating itself and requires action, which interpretation will make you most effective at dealing with that situation?

Challenge yourself. Don't settle for the first interpretation that comes to mind. Say to yourself, "Okay, it might mean that...what else could it mean? What's another way to interpret this?" You will feel better, treat people better, and handle situations better. Do you know what this could mean to you? You tell me.

**Come up with alternative ways
of interpreting an event.**

---

*If you are distressed by anything external,
the pain is not due to the thing itself, but
to your estimate of it; and this you have
the power to revoke at any moment.*

— *Marcus Aurelius*

*Life is 10 percent what you make it
and 90 percent how you take it.*

— *Benjamin Franklin*

Brighter Future?
Sounds Good!

A BRANCH OF PSYCHOLOGY called neurolinguistic programming has made an interesting and useful discovery:
You can change *the way* you imagine or remember things
without changing *what* you imagine, and it will change
your feelings. For example, if a visual memory makes
you sad whenever you think about it, you can make that
mental picture smaller and dimmer, and when you do,
the memory won't make you as sad. Since you haven't
changed the *content* of the memory, you haven't lost any
information. You've simply made it less painful.

When you visually remember a pleasant memory, you
can make the picture more colorful and the memory will
give you even more intense good feelings. You can make
your pictures of the future brighter, wider, deeper, or you

can bring the images closer. Changes like these will make you feel different—even when you leave the *content* of the picture the same.

These are general guidelines. You'll need to experiment for yourself to find out what will work for a particular image. For a few people, making an exciting picture brighter makes the feelings *less* intense. And for some *kinds* of pictures, increasing the brightness would cause the feelings to become less intense—for example, a romantic memory.

What is true for visual images also applies to the way you talk to yourself. For example, if you have trouble motivating yourself, try changing the *tone of voice* you use when you speak to yourself. Some people order themselves around. The voice they use to talk to themselves is harsh and commanding. Listening to *yourself* being bossy can have the same effect as listening to someone else being bossy: It can make you want to rebel. Change your tone to friendly or seductive, and you might feel more motivated. When you tell yourself, "I can do it," fill your internal voice with enthusiasm and back it up with inspiring music. The possibilities are virtually endless.

The important thing to understand is that the way you code your inner world has an impact, and you have quite a bit of control over that coding. You can change it deliberately. When you do, it will change your feelings, which will change your actions, which will change the world around you.

Change the *details* of your thoughts.

Adrift

IN 1982 STEVEN CALLAHAN was crossing the Atlantic alone in his sailboat when it struck something and sank. He was out of the shipping lanes and floating in a life raft, alone. His supplies were few. His chances were small. Yet when three fishermen found him *seventy-six days* later (the longest anyone has survived a shipwreck on a life raft alone), he was alive—much skinnier than he was when he started, but alive.

His account of how he survived is fascinating. His ingenuity—how he managed to catch fish, how he fixed his solar still (evaporates sea water to make fresh)—is very interesting.

But the thing that caught my eye was how he managed to keep himself going when all hope seemed lost, when there seemed no point in continuing the struggle, when he was suffering greatly, when his life raft was punctured and after more than a week struggling with his weak body to fix it, it was still leaking air and wearing him out to keep pumping it up. He was starved. He was desperately dehydrated. He was thoroughly exhausted. Giving up would have seemed the only sane option.

When people *survive* these kinds of circumstances, they do something with their minds that gives them the courage to keep going. Many people in similarly desperate circumstances give in or go mad. Something the survivors do with their thoughts helps them find the guts to carry on in spite of overwhelming odds.

"I tell myself I can handle it," wrote Callahan in his narrative. "Compared to what others have been through, I'm fortunate. I tell myself these things over and over, building up fortitude...."

I wrote that down after I read it. It struck me as something important. And I've told myself the same thing when my own goals seemed far off or when my problems seemed too overwhelming. And every time I've said it, I have always come back to my senses.

The truth is, our circumstances are only bad *compared to* something better. But others *have* been through much worse. I've read enough history to know you and I are lucky to be where we are, when we are, no matter how bad it seems to us compared to our fantasies. It's a sane thought and worth thinking.

So here, coming to us from the extreme edge of survival, are words that can give us strength. Whatever you're going through, tell yourself you can handle it. Compared to what others have been through, you're fortunate. Tell this to yourself over and over, and it will help you get through the rough spots with a little more fortitude.

Tell yourself you can handle it.

---

*If you would only recognize that
life is hard, things would be
so much easier for you.*

— Louis D. Brandeis

*Anyone can hold the helm
when the sea is calm.*

— Publilius Syrus

*...everything can be taken from a man
but one thing: the last of the human
freedoms—to choose one's attitude in
any given set of circumstances...*

— Viktor Frankl

Maybe it's Good

I'D DONE A LOT OF WALKING in the last two days and my feet hurt. Of course, I didn't like it. It's obviously a sign I'm getting old. It's a bad thing. "But maybe it's good," I said to myself, "in fact, maybe it's perfect. Maybe it's strengthening the bones in my feet and when I'm old I'll be able to walk a lot longer."

I don't know how it'll turn out. But since sore feet cause pain, I was automatically against it. But if I knew the pain was doing something good, I would feel different about it. It wouldn't be so bad.

We don't know what the future holds. It is always a possibility that the thing you hate so much right now is something you'll be happy for later. You don't know. *Therefore it is counterproductive to ever pass a negative judgement on* anything *that happens to you.*

It's counterproductive for several reasons: First of all, you don't really *know* if it will turn out in your favor, so passing a negative judgement is putting confidence in an unprovable and possibly false guess. And that, of course, is not straight thinking.

Second, it puts you in a bad mood to pass a negative judgement like that and bad moods are bad for your health, bad for your relationships, and no fun.

Third, according to research at Cornell University, our minds find it easier to *confirm* a judgment than to *dis*confirm it. When you conclude something is bad, your judgment will alter the way you perceive your life in a way that confirms your conclusion.

The good news is, when you judge something as good, your mind works to confirm that judgement also. When you decide "maybe this is something good in disguise," you release the creativity in your brain to *find* ways it's good—not only thinking of new ways to look at the situation, but thinking of ideas you can put into action that will *make* lemonade out of this lemon. When you conclude it's bad, you slam the door on those ways, and they become unavailable to you.

When something happens—anything—before you pass judgment, consider this: It may be *good*.

No matter what happens, assume it's good.

You Can *Change*

STANLEY SCHACHTER WAS PUZZLED. A researcher at Columbia University, Schachter was well versed on the studies of weight-loss and smoking-cessation programs. According to the research, only 10 to 30 percent of the people who participate in those programs are still slender or nonsmoking one year later. Ten to 30 percent. That ain't much.

These studies prompted some researchers and therapists to assert it's nearly impossible to stop smoking or control one's weight permanently.

What puzzled Schachter was that most of the people he knew who wanted to lose weight or quit smoking had somehow been able to do it successfully. He conducted some interviews of his colleagues and friends, and it confirmed his hunch: Those who had tried had succeeded.

He has now spent over twenty years doing research on this, and he has concluded that the key to success in changing long-standing habits is *practice*. According to his research, people who have successfully quit smoking have tried and *failed* a number of times before they finally succeeded. The same was true about losing weight. Apparently you have to *learn* how to keep the change, and after you learn how, it begins to become a new part of yourself that eventually requires very little active effort to maintain.

That's why the studies of weight-loss programs and stop-smoking studies look so bleak: Each is a study of only a single attempt. Schachter found that the more times you go through one of these programs, the more likely the change will be permanent.

So if you have tried to change and failed, try again. And keep trying. You *can* change...and you can learn how to *keep* the change. All you need is practice.

Keep persisting until the change you want happens.

You may have a fresh start any moment
you choose, for this thing we call
"failure" is not the falling down,
but the staying down.

— *Mary Pickford*

The Neutralizer

WHAT'S THE FIRST THING you do when you get a flat tire or when you burn your dinner or when one of your kids gets an F? When something goes wrong, *you say something*—to yourself or to someone else. If you're upset, you think or say emotionally loaded expressions, and *those expressions intensify your upsetting feelings.*

When you find yourself thinking or saying a thought like "This is *terrible*," you can change it to a less emotional description—for example, "This is inconvenient." Notice how different the two statements are, emotionally speaking. Try saying each statement to yourself and check how different they feel.

It seems like a simple change to make, and it is. But it can change a setback from a catastrophe to just annoying, at least in your experience.

The emotionally loaded comment doesn't help you. It may even hinder you from dealing with the situation rationally. The emotionally neutral statement "This is inconvenient," leads to an emotionally neutral response—in other words, a reasonable, practical response.

Try to become emotionally neutral when an emotionally charged response is counterproductive. Notice what you're thinking and try to make the same comment as a bland, computerlike description of the situation rather than a comment charged with emotion.

Instead of "I *hate* her," say "What she did interfered with my personal goals."

Rather than "Oh this is just *great!*" said with a bitter tone of voice, try something like "This isn't very good," said in an emotionless monotone.

Change "#@*!#*#!!" to "I would have preferred it turned out differently."

WHEN YOU'RE SPEAKING to someone, your neutrality can help prevent the other person from getting upset, and it'll keep your own arousal to a minimum.

Instead of complaining to your spouse "I am sick to death of car problems," try something like "Maybe it's time to get another car."

Instead of yelling at your teenage son "I've had it up to *here* with you," how about saying this in an emotionally neutral tone of voice: "I've told you twice not to do that. Next time you do it, I will take away your TV for a week."

NEUTRALIZE THE NEGATIVE. It's a simple technique, but with practice it can level out some of the downturns in this roller-coaster ride we call life without in any way interfering with the upturns.

Describe upsetting situations to yourself in emotionally neutral words.

...practically all human misery and serious emotional turmoil are quite unnecessary...
— *Albert Ellis*

Anything that you have to struggle to do is based on not having yourself organized internally in advance.
— *Richard Bandler*

Stress Control

GETTING CRITICIZED BY YOUR SUPERVISOR; finding out that someone you love has lied to you; receiving some bad news—these things cause stress. And stress has negative consequences, as you well know. But these are only stressful *events*. The source of stress that wreaks the greatest havoc on your health and sanity is ongoing stressful *circumstances*.

Like what? Like when a stepchild moves in with you, permanently disrupting the privacy you had with your spouse; or when your younger brother marries someone who verbally abuses your favorite niece. These are the kinds of stresses you have to *live* with. They don't just come up and rock your world for a little while and then go away. They stay. And, like living in a house with a fire alarm going all day long, it starts to wear you down.

But there is something you can do about it. When you have an ongoing stressful circumstance in your life, you can *modify your level of responsibility.* Either take more responsibility or less. Start by asking yourself, "Am I trying to control something I can't or shouldn't control?" or "Is there something I should take responsibility for that I have been leaving out of my control?"

It might help to write it out. Write the questions and then jot down some ideas—where are you taking too much or too little control of some aspect of your life?

Be specific. You are responsible for your child in general, for example, but *specifically,* do you control what he wears or what he eats or when he goes to bed? You must decide. What exactly do you control and what is either out of your control or none of your business? *You must decide.*

If something is out of your control (or is none of your business and you've been trying to *make* it your business), you will relieve yourself of a lot of stress by letting go of it. Drop that one. Recognize it's out of your control and busy yourself with things that *are* in your control. You may be *in the habit* of trying to control that thing, so you'll have to remind yourself again and again for a couple weeks: "Oh yeah, I'm not trying to control that anymore." Write it on a card and carry it with you. Post notes to yourself on your bathroom mirror. Do whatever you have to do to remember you no longer have to waste your energy trying to control that thing.

Now, if you find something you *should and can* control and haven't been, roll up your sleeves and get to work on solving the problem. Use the problem-solving method from page 226. Deliberately take steps to repair the troubling circumstances. That'll relieve your stress better than anything else. It may be difficult at first; it may actually cause you extra stress to face the situation and try to deal with it, but in the long term, your stress level will go down.

Take responsibility for what you are responsible for, and stop taking responsibility for what is not your responsibility. It's that simple. Control what you can control, and let the rest go. It will relieve a great deal of your stress. Control stress by stressing control.

Control what is your responsibility.

There comes a time in the affairs of men
when you must take the bull by the tail
and face the situation.

— W.C. Fields

The Old Switcheroo

WE ALL HAVE TIMES WHEN we think about something negative we can't do anything about: Something in the news, something that happened yesterday, one of our fellow workers who made us mad, a company policy. The time spent ruminating on that stuff is wasted. It's *worse* than wasted, because it makes our bodies produce stress hormones, which circulate in the bloodstream and aren't good for our health.

When you find yourself thinking about something negative and you want to stop, I'd like to give you a technique...but I can't. The mind doesn't work that way. It's like a river that just keeps flowing, and even when you try to dam it up, it just overflows the dam and keeps on flowing. A river *must* flow. You can't stop it.

But you *can* redirect it.

The same is true for your mind. It keeps flowing; it keeps thinking. You can't stop it. But you *can* redirect it.

When you are thinking about something negative you can't do anything about, redirect your mind. There are a million things you could direct your mind to, but let's choose a good one now rather than wait until we're bothered by something. Here's an extremely useful area to redirect your mind to: *Complimenting other people.*

You and I know we take things for granted and it would be good to appreciate what people do for us, but we don't, at least not as often as we'd like. Why? Because we need to *think* about it. When we compliment someone without giving it any thought, it comes out shallow, general, or phony. To do it well requires *thought.*

But we don't have the spare time to think about it— we're too busy thinking about negative things we can't do anything about (wink).

So from this point on, use the occurrence of needless negative rumination as a trigger—something that reminds you to think about complimenting someone. Use it as an opportunity to switch your mind, to turn it in a new direction. What specifically has someone done that you think was cool? Big or small, it doesn't matter. Next time you see that person, let them know you appreciate it. The fact that you acknowledge it some time after it happens shows it was important enough for you to think about later, which adds more impact to the compliment.

Give more sincere and well-thought-out compliments and your relationships will be better, your life will be better, the world will be better. And one way to give more compliments is to use the old switcheroo.

When you want to stop ruminating about something:
**Direct your thoughts to what
you appreciate and say it.**

---

*The measure of mental health is the
disposition to find good everywhere.*

— *Ralph Waldo Emerson*

*Silent gratitude isn't much use
to anyone.*

— *Gladys Browyn Stern*

*I like not only to be loved, but to be told that
I am loved; the realm of silence is large
enough beyond the grave.*

— *Publilius Syrus*

Having the Time

I WAS JUST READING A TRUE STORY about a Norwegian soldier who had been put out of action by frostbite and was confined to a small sled in the middle of the Arctic wilderness. Some friends were hiding him from the German soldiers who were occupying Norway. He was alone for twenty-seven days except for a short visit by someone about every three or four days. He had a book with him, but he didn't read much of it during those twenty-seven days. He "never seemed to have the time."

When I read that last line, it jolted me awake and has been bugging me ever since. Do you understand why? Here was a man who couldn't walk, who was confined to a sleeping bag in the middle of a silent, snow-covered, completely uninhabited area in the Arctic, and he was too busy to read. What's wrong with this picture?

What's wrong is the same thing that's wrong with you and me. We're too busy. You are, aren't you? Yeah, so am I. Short of time. More things to do than you have time to do. Always trying to catch up.

But what has been dawning on me with a certain degree of irony and ridiculousness is that my lack of time is completely created by me.

There is no shortage of time. There is only the greedy effort to get more from our days than we can, while at the same time greedily wanting to also spend some of that time in leisure.

It's silly. And it's tragic. It costs us the experience of living. Time seems to fly by. Wow, where did those last ten years go? Were we so busy getting things done we forgot to enjoy our own lives?

Let's just relax, shall we? Let's quit trying to do so much. We don't *have* to get all that stuff done. We don't *have* to be perfect parents—kids have been raised by imperfect parents for a long time and still turned out okay. We don't have to be perfect at anything. We don't have to do it all. And we don't have to be happier. But when we realize we don't have to cram so much into our days, we will be.

If your own greed is making you discontent, quit cramming so much into your days.

Think Positive—
Positively!

WHEN A PERSON THINKS A NEGATIVE THOUGHT and *tries to get rid of it,* that person is thinking positively negatively. Daniel M. Wegner of Trinity University in San Antonio, Texas, has conducted a long string of experiments that show the futility and actual danger of trying to get rid of thoughts.

In some of the experiments, Wegner told his subjects, "Try not to think about a white bear." The subjects were then asked to say aloud everything that came to mind. Of course, thoughts of white bears showed up quite a bit. Trying *not* to think of a white bear produced a thought of a white bear between six and fifteen times in a five-minute period.

Trying *not* to think a negative thought will result in thinking it *more*.

Thinking is like breathing: It goes on night and day and you can't stop it. But you *can* change it. You can breathe slowly and deeply or shallowly and quickly. You can breathe any way you want. But you can't *stop*.

The same is true about thinking. You can say something stupid or depressing to yourself; you can say something intelligent or inspiring to yourself; but you can't stop thinking entirely.

So when you find yourself disliking the content of your thoughts, instead of trying to *stop* yourself from thinking a thought, try to *direct* your thoughts.

And the way to direct your thinking is by *asking yourself a question*. A question gets your mind going in a new direction without suppressing what you're already thinking. Ask yourself a question.

Of course, the *kind* of question you ask makes a big difference. If you ask "Why is this happening to poor me?" your answers won't help you any.

The idea is to direct your mind by asking questions that put your attention on practical things, on accomplishment, on the future. If you find yourself worrying, for example, ask yourself something like this: "How can I make myself stronger and better able to deal with this?" Or "Can I get busy right now working on my goal—so busy I forget all about my worries? And if not, is there some planning I can do now that will save me time later?" Or even simply "What is my goal?"

When you find yourself thinking negatively about something "bad" that happened, ask yourself "What's good about this?" Or "How can I turn this to my advantage?" Or "What assumption have I made that I can argue with?" Ask a good question.

When you decide on a question to ask yourself, ask the question and *keep asking*. Ponder it. Wonder about it. Let it run through your mind whenever your mind isn't otherwise engaged. It will turn the tide of your thoughts and bring you into a new state of mind because you're thinking positively *positively*.

**Direct your mind by asking yourself
a good question.**

---

*I have learned that most of the time you
can't fight and you can't flee, but you can
learn to flow.*

— *Robert S. Eliot, MD*

*Whatever your present environment
may be, you will fall, remain or rise
with your thoughts.*

— *James Allen*

The Uncertainty Principle

TWO SAILORS RAN INTO EACH OTHER in a pub. Over a few beers, one of the men told the other about his last voyage: "After a month at sea," he said, "we discovered our masts had been eaten through by termites! Almost nothing left of them."

"That's terrible," said the second sailor.

"That's what I thought at first too," the first sailor said, "but it turned out to be good luck. As soon as we took the sails down to fix the masts, we were hit by a squall so suddenly and so hard, it would surely have blown us over if our sails were up at the time."

"How lucky!"

"That's exactly what I thought at the time too. But because our sails were down, we couldn't steer ourselves, and because of the wind, we were blown onto a reef. The hole in the hull was too big to fix. We were stranded."

"That is bad luck indeed."

"That's what I thought, too, when it first happened. But we all made it to the beach alive and had plenty to eat. But now here's the real kicker: While we were on the island whining about our terrible fate, we discovered a buried treasure!"

As this story illustrates, you don't know if an event is "good" or "bad" except maybe in retrospect, and even *then* you don't really know because *life keeps going.* The story's not over yet. Just because something hasn't turned out to be an advantage *yet* doesn't mean it is not ever *going* to.

Therefore, you can simply *assume* whatever happens is "good."

I know that sounds awfully airy-fairy, but it's very practical. If you think an event is good, it's easy to maintain a positive attitude. And your attitude affects your health, it affects the way people treat you and how you treat others, and it affects your energy level. And those can help pave the way for things to turn out well. A good attitude is a good thing. And a bad attitude does you no good at all.

So get in the habit of saying "That's good!" Since you don't know for sure whether something will eventually work to your advantage or not, you might as well *assume it will.* It is counterproductive to assume otherwise. Think about it.

If someone ahead of you in line at a store is slowing everything down, say to yourself, "That's good!" They may have saved you from getting into an accident when you get back in your car. Or maybe because you slowed down, you might meet a friend you would have missed. You never know.

The truth is, life is uncertain. And even *that* can work to your advantage.

**When something "bad" happens,
say to yourself, "That's good!"**

---

*There are no circumstances, no matter how
unfortunate, that clever people do not extract
some advantage from; and none, no matter
how fortunate, that the unwise cannot turn to
their own disadvantage.*

— *Francois de La Rochefoucauld*

*A pessimist is one who makes difficulties
of his opportunities; an optimist makes
opportunities of his difficulties.*

— *Reginald B. Mansell*

Unpleasant Feelings

NEGATIVE FEELINGS PLAGUE all of us from time to time. Worry creeps into the mind like an unwelcome in-law, and if something isn't done about it, the worry will stay and eat you out of house and home. Anger strikes, pumping your body full of adrenaline, making it hard to concentrate on your work or speak with a civil tongue. Depression brings feelings of hopelessness and helplessness, darkening and saddening your world like a cold, bleak day in winter.

These are the three faces of negative feelings: Worry, anger, depression. Most negative feelings you ever feel are a shade of anxiety, anger, or sadness. You know these feelings are unpleasant. You know they aren't good for your health. But what can you do to minimize the amount of time you feel them?

First, of course, is to look at the situation causing the negative feelings. If there is a concrete circumstance, a real problem causing the feeling, give it some good hard thought and then do something about it, if you can.

But if there's nothing you can do about it, get involved in something that engages your mind and forget about it. Don't try to stop thinking negatively. Simply try to get absorbed in doing something constructive.

Purposeful activities occupy mind-space, and the more the task engages or takes up your attention, the more mind-space it occupies. Get involved enough in something or do something absorbing enough, and there's no more mind-space left to think about anything else.

What continues a negative emotion is *thinking* about it. Just as you can distract a crying child and he will forget his skinned knee, you can distract yourself with something so interesting or challenging or important, your mind will stop thinking about the problem, and your negative feelings—now that you're no longer producing them with your thoughts—will dissipate.

Seek escape from unnecessary negative feelings by fleeing into a purpose. It will take your mind off the negative thing, giving you a healthful break from those negative feelings. The side effect is that something purposeful and productive gets done in the meantime. And that will give you something to feel *good* about.

Relieve negative feelings by turning your attention to purposeful activities.

The How of Tao

THE ATTITUDE OF TAOISM and the Buddhist concept of nonattachment and the basic principle of cognitive therapy can be reduced to a single technique that creates calm, contentment, and peace of mind. The technique is to let go of an idea you're clinging to. Remind yourself it is only an idea and stop clinging to it as if the idea were meaningful and weighty.

For example, Judy is a thirty-eight-year-old woman who lives in the same town as her alcoholic mother. Judy was upset about this. It bothered her that her mother drank so much every day. One day she discovered the prime source of her stress: The idea that it was her *duty* to save her mom.

So she gave up the idea. It was just an *idea*, after all, it was not The Law. And the idea caused her needless suffering. So every time she felt upset because of her mother's drinking, she said to herself: *The only one who can stop Mom's drinking is Mom.* She became happier, more relaxed, and probably healthier.

She let go of a fixed notion that she *should* save her mom. Giving up an attachment to an idea is known by Buddhists and Taoists as *nonattachment.* It is known by cognitive therapists as *arguing against "should" statements.* And in Rational-Emotive Therapy, they call it *giving up musturbation.* Clinging to an idea is the source of the bulk of human suffering.

Here's the technique:

1. When you notice yourself unhappy about something, ask yourself what *idea* you are grasping, clinging to, clutching.

2. Say to yourself, "This is just an idea, and ideas are not reality. This idea doesn't help me, so I'll no longer use it as a guide. The idea is now dismissed, thank you very much."

3. When the idea comes back later—as it probably will—dismiss it again. You may be in the *habit* of thinking the idea, so it'll come up again after you've dismissed it, like an idiot employee who doesn't understand he has already been fired. Send him home again. And again. And as

many times as you must until he eventually stops coming back.

YOU WILL RELAX and feel happier every time you let go of an idea that has been causing you unnecessary stress.

Let go of an idea that causes you needless stress.

People sometimes think of Buddhism as a negative religion...but when we can let go without turning away we find the secret of joy and love. Energy springs up, which is not exhausted by clinging and defending...

— Dhiravamsa

Assume that every time you really feel anxious, depressed, or angry you are not only strongly desiring *but also* commanding *that something go well and that you get what you want.*

— Albert Ellis

Pillar of Strength

IN HIS BOOK *GRINDING IT OUT*, Ray Kroc, the man who made McDonald's what it is today, wrote about his father. Kroc senior was a hard-working man who was doing well in real estate before the Depression, expanding his holdings and using credit to extend himself even further. "When the market collapsed, he was crushed beneath a pile of deeds he could not sell," wrote Kroc. "The land they described was worth less than he owed. This was an unbearable situation for a man of my father's principled conservatism. He died of a cerebral hemorrhage in 1930. He had worried himself to death. On his desk the day he died were two pieces of paper—his last paycheck from the telegraph company and a garnishment notice for the entire amount of his wages."

Bad stuff happens, and sometimes it's big. You don't want it to crush you. You want to be strong. So start now taking every small bad thing that happens as an opportunity to repeat this idea to yourself:

There will be an advantage in this. I will find it or I will make it.

REPEAT IT UNTIL you see or can make an advantage out of it. If you will do this, you will stand as a fortress of strength for your family in situations that would make lesser men and women collapse in hopelessness. This idea is not some namby-pamby, rah-rah, positive-thinking nonsense. It is a source of tremendous strength. It may save your life some day. For sure it will be good for your health. Ingrain that thought—make that pathway through your brain well-worn—and you'll be able to face up to difficulties that would make a mere mortal crawl and whimper.

Arnold Schwarzenegger is more successful than most people know. He's made a lot of money with his films and married a Kennedy, but he's also a smart and successful businessman outside of the movie business, with real estate, books, restaurants, and fitness clubs. He is hugely successful. In his autobiography, he wrote,

I didn't get certain things I needed as a child, and that, I think, finally made me hungry for achievement...If I'd gotten everything and been well-balanced, I wouldn't have had my drive. [Because of] this negative element in my up-bringing, I had a positive drive toward success...

HE HELD UP under the strain and turned it to his advantage. He didn't let it crush him *because of the way he thinks.* This strength is within your grasp: Find or make an advantage in everything that happens.

Find a way to turn your problems into an advantage.

When one door of happiness closes, another opens; but often we look so long at the closed door that we do not see the one which has opened for us.

— *Helen Keller*

There is no fruit which is not bitter before it is ripe.

— *Publilius Syrus*

Meanings and Feelings

STANLEY SCHACHTER SET UP the following experiment: He first divided his experimental subjects into two groups and gave them all a shot of adrenaline. Then the subjects mingled with Schachter's assistants, whom the subjects had been led to believe were given a shot too.

In one group, the assistants acted as if they were experiencing anxiety. In the other group, the assistants acted excited and happy. Asked what the shot had done to them, subjects in the first group said the adrenaline shot made them feel anxious; subjects in the second group said the adrenaline made them feel excited and elated.

The way the assistants acted influenced the way the subjects interpreted their experience. And it was their *interpretations* that made their experience pleasant or unpleasant. The adrenaline shot was the same in both groups, and caused the same effects: it made their hearts pound, dilated their eyes, sent glucose to the muscles, and shut down the digestive tract.

Both groups experienced the same *physical* changes, but the way the assistants acted created a different *meaning* for the physical changes, and those meanings made the difference between anxiety and elation.

Change the *meaning* of an experience and the experience changes.

The late Viktor Frankl, a psychiatrist and a survivor of Hitler's concentration camps, often changed the meaning of events for his patients, and it changed their lives. For example, an elderly and severely depressed man came to see Frankl. His wife had died and she had meant more to him than anything in the world.

"What would have happened," Frankl asked the man, "if you had died first, and your wife would have survived you?"

The man answered: "Oh, for her this would have been terrible; how she would have suffered!"

"You see," said Frankl, "such a suffering has been spared her, and it is *you* who have spared her this suffering; but now, you have to pay for it by surviving and mourning her."

The man didn't say anything. He shook Dr. Frankl's hand and calmly left. Frankl wrote:

Suffering ceases to be suffering in some way at the moment it finds a meaning, such as the meaning of a sacrifice.

THE MEANINGS YOU make in your life can be the difference between anxiety and elation, between hopelessness and courage, between failure and success, and even, as Frankl discovered in the concentration camps, between living and dying.

You have some control over the way you interpret the events of your life. The meanings of events are not written in stone. You can create more useful meanings for yourself. All it takes is a little thought.

Interpret events in a way that helps you.

Be not afraid of life. Believe that life is worth living, and your belief will help create the fact.

— William James

The Great Way is not difficult—just cease to cherish opinions.

— The Third Zen Patriarch

Expect the Best

NOELLE CAME TO WORK worried about her roommate, Jana, who didn't come home the night before and didn't call. That wasn't like Jana, and Noelle was worried.

But Noelle's worry did not benefit Jana, and it harmed Noelle. Worry put stress hormones into her bloodstream, which isn't healthy. It suppressed her immune system. If she worries a lot, it will damage the inside of her arteries, which can end in a heart attack or stroke many years hence. Needless worry is a cost without a benefit. And it's not pleasant.

If you are worrying and want to stop, first ask yourself if there's anything you're going to do about the situation. If not, then start wondering what good things might be happening. *Do not try to stop worrying.*

Research by Daniel Wegner, PhD, of the University of Virginia has repeatedly shown that trying to suppress thoughts only results in thinking the thought more. If you try to suppress a thought hard enough, that thought can become an obsession.

Try to stop worrying and you'll worry even more. What you want to do is give your mind a bone to chew on, but a *different* bone. Worrying is imagining something bad happening. Simply imagine something good happening, and there will be less room in your mind for imagining something bad happening. Your mind has its limits, like the RAM of a computer. Give it enough to do, and it won't have the free space to do anything else.

If worrying is a habit for you, it won't go away immediately. Every time you start to worry, ask yourself what good might be happening. And keep asking and wondering and then leave it at that—an open-ended possibility. Do this and something good will be happening to *you*: You'll feel better and you'll be healthier.

By the way, Jana had a wonderful time.

Wonder about what *good* things might be happening.

Worry is a dark room where fears are developed and enlarged.

— Teresa Eagel

Blind Spots

COVER YOUR LEFT EYE, hold this page close to you, and look at the X. As you slowly pull the book away from you, at some point the 0 will disappear. Or cover your right eye and look at the 0, and pull the book away, and the X will disappear.

X   0

YOU HAVE A blind spot in each eye where the bundles of nerve fibers go back into your brain. But notice something: *You don't see the blind spot.* It doesn't show up like a dark, empty spot. Your brain fills in the emptiness.

In a similar way, when there is *information* you don't know, *your brain fills it in*, giving you the feeling that nothing is missing. In other words, when you feel certain, it doesn't really mean much. Your feeling of certainty doesn't necessarily have any relationship to your actual correctness or knowledge. Your brain produces a feeling of certainty at the drop of a hat because it's wired up to do so.

All human brains tend to jump to conclusions and then feel certain about those conclusions, so it pays to be somewhat skeptical of your own mind. That may seem like a negative goal, but it isn't. Feeling certain has caused more problems for people than skepticism ever did.

For example, when you're arguing with your spouse, the thing that keeps the anger intense is that you're both *certain* you're right. If each of you had a little more skepticism about your own ability to remember and reason, it would be easier to work out your differences.

To take another example, depressed people would get depressed less often if they became more skeptical of the pessimistic assumptions they make. The *feeling of certainty* depressed people have about their own pessimistic view of the world does them harm.

Don't place much importance in your feelings of certainty. Be skeptical. Recognize you have blind spots and act accordingly. You'll be saner if you do.

Be skeptical of your feelings of certainty.

Fighting Spirit

MARTIN SELIGMAN, PHD, and his research team tested the swim team of the University of California at Berkeley to find out who were optimists and who were pessimists. Then they created a setback for the team members: The coach told each swimmer his time after he finished a heat, but the coach didn't give the swimmer an accurate time—he gave a time much *slower* than the swimmer's real time.

How did the swimmers respond do this setback? Seligman says, "The optimists responded by swimming their next heat *faster*; the pessimists went *slower* on their next heat."

Optimists fight back when they hit a setback. They are resilient in the face of the rejections and disappointments we all face at one time or another in our lives. Optimists pick themselves up quickly and go on. They bounce back.

Pessimists succumb. They give up. They get depressed. They throw in the towel and let life run them over. And the only thing that separates optimists from pessimists is *the way they think*—called their "explanatory style." When optimists have setbacks:

1. They assume the problem or its consequences won't last very long.

2. They don't indulge in self-blame. Instead they look to see if there's anything they could do to prevent the same thing from happening in the future.

3. They don't jump to the conclusion that this setback will ruin *everything.* An optimist will try to see how much of their lives the setback won't affect.

YOU CAN BECOME more optimistic by practicing these three ways of thinking about setbacks, and every inch you move toward optimism means another inch of resiliency. It means you'll bounce back sooner from the inevitable setbacks of life. It means you'll have greater personal strength and persistence. It means more of your life will go the way you want it to go.

Look at those three optimistic ways of thinking. Find the one you're weakest in and work on it. Practice on the little setbacks you experience—the small disappointments, frustrations, annoyances, interruptions in your everyday experience. Learn to think the optimistic way. Practice until that way of thinking is habitual.

When it seems like life is trying to beat you down, fight back with optimistic thoughts.

When you hit a setback in life:
Assume the problem or its consequences won't last long, see how you can prevent the same problem in the future, and don't jump to the conclusion that this setback will ruin everything.

Explanatory style...can produce depression in response to everyday setbacks, or produce resilience even in the face of tragedy.
It can numb a person to the pleasures of life, or allow him to live fully.
It can prevent him from achieving his goals, or help him exceed them.

— Martin Seligman

How to Improve Your Self-Esteem

SELF-ESTEEM IS SELF-WORTH or self-value. So to increase your self-esteem, increase your worth or value. A lot of people would interpret that to mean "change the way you think about your worth or value." But I mean change what you *do* in order to make yourself worth more—to yourself and others. Make yourself worth more *in reality*, not just in your mind.

How? Here are four ways to go about it:

1. **Gain more ability**. If you are a manager, you could take classes or read books to increase your ability to manage. If you live in fear of physical harm, you could take a self-defense class. Become more able to do what needs to be done.

2. **Become more honest**. Every person has been dishonest. And you know it feels bad. It doesn't make us feel good about ourselves. Every effort you make, no matter how small, to become more honest will make you worth more to yourself. It will increase your personal pride in a healthy way.

3. **Do something worthwhile**. Are you doing something worthwhile? That depends on what I mean by "worthwhile," doesn't it? No! It depends on what *you* consider worthwhile. In order to feel self-worth, you need to know you're doing something worthwhile. Otherwise, your self-worth would be a sham. So spend some time wondering what that worthwhile task might be for you. It is a worthwhile pursuit to find a worthwhile pursuit!

4. **Acknowledge people**. Try to give three good acknowledgments a day. It's a whole new way of life. And it will increase *your* self-esteem.

ALL FOUR OF these things improve your value and worth, to yourself and other people. And that's what self-esteem is all about.

To increase your own self-esteem:
**Gain more ability, become more honest,
do something worthwhile,
and acknowledge people.**

All in Your Head

IN 1914, A SMALL SHIP SAILED into the icy Weddell Sea, on its way to the South Pole. It carried a crew of twenty-seven men, and their leader, Ernest Shackleton. But unseasonable gales shoved the floating ice together and the temperature sank below zero, freezing more than a million square miles of ice into a solid mass. And they were stuck in the middle of it. They had no radio transmitter. They were alone.

For ten months the pressure increased until it crushed the ship, stranding them in the middle of an icy wasteland which could, at any time, break up and become a sea of floating ice chunks. They had to get off this ice while it was still solid, so they headed for the nearest known land, *346 miles away*, dragging their two lifeboats over the ice. But every few hundred yards they ran into a pressure ridge, sometimes two stories high, caused by the ice compacting. They had to chop through it. At the end of two backbreaking days in subzero weather, they were exhausted. After all their hacking and dragging, they had traveled only two miles.

They tried again. In five days they went a total of nine miles, but the ice was becoming softer and the pressure ridges were becoming larger. They could go no further. So they had to wait...for several *months*. Finally the ice opened up and they launched the boats into the churning mass of giant chunks of ice and made it out. But now they were sailing across a treacherous sea. They landed on a tiny, barren, ice-covered, lifeless island in the middle of nowhere.

To save themselves, they needed to reach the nearest outpost of civilization: South Georgia, *870 miles away!* Shackleton and five men took the best lifeboat and sailed across the Drake Passage at the tip of South America, the most formidable piece of ocean in the world. Gales blow nonstop—up to 200 miles an hour (that's as hard as a hurricane)—and waves get as high as ninety feet. Their chances of making it were very close to zero.

But determination can change the odds.

They made it. But they landed on the wrong side of the island, and their boat was pounded into the rocks and rendered useless. The whaling port they needed to reach was on the other side of the island, which has peaks 10,000 feet high and had never been crossed. They were the first. They didn't have much choice.

When they staggered into the little whaling port on the other side of the island, everyone who saw them stopped dead in their tracks. The three men had coal-black skin from the seal oil they had been burning as fuel. They had long, black dreadlocks. Their clothing was shredded, filthy rags, and they had come from the direction of the mountains. Nobody in the history of the whaling port had ever been known to enter the town from that direction.

Although all the men at that whaling port had known about Shackleton's expedition, his ship had been gone for seventeen months and was assumed to have sunk, and the crew with it. The whalers knew how deadly and unforgiving the ice could be.

The three ragged men made their way to the home of a man Shackleton knew, followed in silence by a growing crowd of people. When the man came to the door, he stepped back and stared in silence. Then he said, "Who the hell are you?"

The man in the center took a step forward and said, "My name is Shackleton."

According to some witnesses, the hard-faced man at the door turned away and wept.

This story is incredible, and if it weren't for the extensive verification and corroboration of the diaries and interviews with the men on the crew in Alfred Lansing's account, *Endurance*, it might easily be disbelieved. The story is true, and as incredible as what I've told you seems, I've only given you some highlights.

Shackleton went back and rescued his friends on the other side of the island first, and then after many attempts to get through the ice, on August 30th—almost two *years* since they'd embarked—he made it back to that barren island and rescued the rest of his men. Every man in Shackleton's crew made it home alive.

Fifteen years earlier, a different ship got stuck in the ice in the Weddell Sea—the *Belgica*, led by Adrien de Gerlache—but they didn't do so well. During the winter in the Antarctic, the sun completely disappears below the horizon for seventy-nine days. Shackleton's crew endured it. But the crew of the *Belgica* grew depressed, gave up hope, and succumbed to negative thinking. Some of them couldn't eat. Mental illness took over. One man had a heart attack from a terror of darkness. Paranoia and hysteria ran rampant.

None of this happened to Shackleton's men because he insisted they keep a good attitude, and he did the same. He once said that the most important quality for an explorer was not courage or patience, but *optimism*. He said, "Optimism nullifies disappointment and makes one more ready than ever to go on."

Shackleton also knew that attitudes are contagious. He was fully aware of the fact that if anyone lost hope they wouldn't be able to put forth that last ounce of energy which may make the difference. And they *did* get pushed to the limits of human endurance. But he had convinced himself and his men they would make it out alive. His determination to remain optimistic ultimately saved their lives.

And it can achieve great things for you too. It comes down to what you say: Either *you* say it's hopeless or *you* say it can be done. You can never look into the future to find the answer. It's in your head.

Make up your mind you will succeed.

Every noble work is, at first, impossible.

— Thomas Carlyle

Persistence and determination alone are omnipotent. The slogan "press on" has solved and always will solve the problems of the human race.

— Calvin Coolidge

History has demonstrated that the most notable winners usually encountered heartbreaking obstacles before they triumphed. They won because they refused to become discouraged by their defeats.

— B.C. Forbes

Think Strong

SOME PEOPLE ARE EMOTIONALLY stronger than others. They can take a lot of stress and strain without falling apart, while others collapse into a whimpering heap at the smallest things.

The main difference between an emotionally weak person and an emotionally strong person is *what they think when things go wrong*. When troubles come along, the weak one is in the habit of thinking: "This is more than I can stand." A tough one thinks: "I can handle this."

It doesn't matter what specific words a person puts to the two different kinds of thinking. But the thoughts that make people weak are feeble and impotent: "I can't take it, it's too overwhelming, it's too much to bear, I can't stand it, I'm not up to this, I'm not emotionally ready for this," etc.

The thoughts that make you strong are capable and resolute: "I can take it, everything is going to work out, I'll get through it, maybe there's a lesson in it for me, adversity builds character, I'm tough, people have been through worse, if I try I can find an advantage in all this, when this is over I'll be wiser," etc.

To become stronger, change your thoughts. It's as simple and uncomplicated as that. There's nothing to it but to do it. Start saying something different to yourself during tough times. When you feel stress, coach yourself, "Come on, [your name here], you can handle this. When this is over, you might even be a stronger person because of it." Think strong thoughts and you will be tougher, braver, and more resilient. Just like that.

The stronger thoughts are *truer* than the weak thoughts. You *can* take it. Human beings, including you, can withstand a tremendous amount of strain without cracking, as any cursory perusal of war stories, survival accounts, and reports of disasters demonstrate.

These kinds of thoughts won't be habitual at first, of course. The way you think is as much a habit as the way you tie your shoes. But keep deliberately thinking stronger, and after awhile it will become habitual. Eventually, you'll wonder how you ever thought differently.

Would you like to be stronger? Would you like to have more emotional calm during the stressful times? Would you like to stand as a pillar of strength when those about you are crumbling? Sure you would. This is the way. Change your thoughts. Make them stronger. Don't think you can do it? That's the first thought to change.

**Think thoughts that give you strength
and make you tough.**

If I were asked to give...advice for all humanity it would be this: Expect trouble as an inevitable part of life and when it comes, hold your head high, look it squarely in the eye and say, "I will be bigger than you. You cannot defeat me."

— *Ann Landers*

Happy, satisfied persons control their mental attitude. They take a positive view of their situation. They look for the good, and when something isn't so good, they look first to themselves to see if they can improve it.

— *Napoleon Hill and W. Clement Stone*

Where to Tap

EVER HEAR THE STORY of the giant ship engine that failed? The ship's owners tried one expert after another, but none of them could figure out how to fix the engine. Then they brought in an old man who had been fixing ships since he was a youngster. He carried a large bag of tools with him, and when he arrived, he immediately went to work. He inspected the engine very carefully, top to bottom. Two of the ship's owners were there, watching this man, hoping he would know what to do. After looking things over, the old man reached into his bag and pulled out a small hammer. He gently tapped something.

Instantly, the engine lurched into life. He carefully put his hammer away. The engine was fixed!

A week later, the owners received a bill from the old man for ten thousand dollars.

"What?!" the owners exclaimed. "He hardly did anything!" So they wrote the old man a note saying, "Please send us an itemized bill."

The man sent a bill that read,

Tapping with a hammer..................................$2
Knowing where to tap...............................$9998

Effort is important, but knowing *where* to make an effort in your life makes all the difference. And here's something I've learned from experience and study: If you want to improve your life overall, the best place to tap is *exercise*.

I injured a tendon not too long ago and didn't exercise for about a month. I've started again, and I've become a born-again exerciser! I'd forgotten how good it is for my sense of well-being. I have more energy, a better attitude, a gentler disposition. It's easier to be the kind of person I want to be.

Our bodies *need* daily exercise, and when we don't exercise, it makes us feel bad. I think it's our natural state to be energetic and feeling good. But the lack of exercise prevents that.

A consensus is building among doctors, psychologists and those trying to help others become saner, happier and healthier: Exercise is the place to start. If you were in a position to give advice, and someone unhappy or unhealthy came to you for guidance but you were allowed to give only one word of advice, the best thing you could recommend is: Exercise!

Exercise regularly.

Following 32,000 people for eight years, [Steven Blair] found that those whose only risk [factor] was inactivity were more likely to die prematurely than those who had high cholesterol, high blood pressure, AND a smoking habit but who got some exercise each day.

— Katherine Griffin

We age because of deterioration rather than deteriorate because of aging.

— Douglas Baumber

All ten studies confirmed that exercise significantly reduces mild to moderate depression. And the three studies that compared exercise to psychotherapy found that exercise was at least as effective.

— Consumer Reports on Health

A Simple Way to Change How You Feel

SOMETIMES WHEN YOU WANT to *behave* differently, you don't *feel* like it when the time comes. And sometimes when you want to *feel* differently, you don't really know how to get there from where you are. Maybe you want to feel confident talking with strangers or feel cheerful at work, but you don't know *how* to feel confident or cheerful. Well, there is a way.

The principle is simple: Assume the posture you would have if you felt the way you want to feel, breathe the way you would breathe, talk the way you would talk, think the things you would think, act the way you would act—do the things you would do if you felt the way you want to feel.

Are you depressed and want to feel happy? Move your body like you move it when you're happy. If you can't remember what it's like to be happy, move your body the same way you've seen others move when they looked happy. Put the same expression on your face. Imagine or remember the way you talk to yourself and the kind of perspective you might have about your situation when you're happy, and then say those things to yourself and take that perspective.

In other words, *act as though* you were happy.

If you are angry and want to be calm, *act as though* you were calm. Do you feel weak and want to be strong? *Act as though* you were strong.

What you're doing is changing everything that *can* be changed, and this changes your feelings, which can't be changed directly.

Remember Pavlov's dogs? Pavlov rang a bell every time he fed the dogs, and the dogs associated the sound of the bell with the taste of food. So when the bell rang, the dogs salivated, even when there was no food.

For your whole life you've been relating certain body postures, facial expressions, breathing patterns, etc., to certain feelings like happiness or calmness or strength. The postures and facial expressions and feelings belong together. So when you act as though you're relaxed, you begin to feel relaxed. When you act as though you feel good, you begin to feel good. And after awhile, you aren't acting. It's like siphoning gas—you suck on the hose at first, and then it comes out by itself.

"Acting as though" also changes reality, which tends to reinforce the feelings. For example, people who feel depressed typically aren't very friendly. If they acted like a person who felt good, they would act friendlier, which would cause people to act friendly in return, which would make the person feel less depressed. It creates an upward spiral. Change how you act and what you do and your feelings will change. You will get a better response from the world, which will reinforce your good feelings.

Act as though you already feel the way you *want* to feel.

You are more likely to act yourself into feeling than to feel yourself into acting.

— *Jerome Bruner*

Action seems to follow feeling, but really action and feeling go together; and by regulating the action, which is under the more direct control of the will, we can indirectly regulate the feeling, which is not.

— *William James*

We've Been Duped

PEOPLE FELT RICHER in the 1950s—when houses averaged 1100 square feet—than they do now, when they average 2000 square feet. There were no VCRs, no microwaves, no cable TV, no PCs, no video games, hardly any dishwashers, and in most homes only the father brought in an income. Yet according to surveys, our reported level of happiness peaked in 1957 and has gone down as our level of wealth has gone up.

The reason is simple: You and I don't need much to be happy. Most of us are doing too much, working too hard, trying to make "enough" money. But it costs us time. And after a certain point—a point we have all passed a long time ago—you get less and less happiness for more and more expenditure of time to earn money. And that is time taken away from time spent with your loved ones, where a good deal of happiness *does* come from. Those moments of simple human interaction—talking, playing a game, taking a walk, cooking together—those are the real riches of life.

You've been exposed to barrage of advertising, something like a million ads by the time you're twenty. And those advertising people are experts on human nature. They've read all the studies showing what influences people, and they carefully design their advertisements to pull your attention and then to convince you their product would make you happy. They have been trying to manipulate your values since you were a kid. They've been trying to get you to believe *having* things is what will make you happy.

Most of us are way too busy, and that's just perfect as far as the advertisers are concerned. We're out working to earn more money so we have more to spend on products. If we would learn to curb our desire for so much stuff, we wouldn't have to work as much, so we'd be able to spend more unscheduled time with our loved ones.

You already know this, I'm sure. But the more you hear something the more of an impact it will make on your feelings and behavior. Ask any advertiser.

You want more time? You want more enjoyment? There is a way, but it will require a little discipline: *Do without*. You'll be a lot richer.

Remind yourself you don't need much to be happy.

How to Like Yourself More

IT'S IMPOSSIBLE TO LIKE YOURSELF much when you're doing something you think is wrong. It doesn't matter how much rationalization you do, or how thickly you try to cover it with justification, if you think it's wrong or bad, and you keep doing it, you cannot like yourself. So the way to like yourself more is to clean up your integrity. You may not like to hear that, and I don't blame you. It sounds like a horrible burden. But it's not. It lightens your load and makes it more fun to be alive. Here are three steps to a self you like and respect.

1. **Make a list of what you're doing that you think is wrong and stop doing those things.** You might keep backsliding for awhile, but if

you keep at it, you'll make it. Also make a list of things you should be doing and aren't. Never mind what others think you should or shouldn't do or what you've been told is right or wrong. Just pay attention to what *you feel* is right or wrong. And make sure you *write it out*. This, by itself, will give you some relief, because we are never as bad as we think we are. When you write it out, you'll see that. The list will be finite. Work on one thing at a time. Then cross it off your list.

2. **Make amends for anything you've done in the past that you feel guilty about.** Some situations only need an apology, or just an admission that you did it. Other situations will require you to *take some action* to make up for the damage you did. Before you get started on this, you should know that it's never as bad as you think it will be. It's easier to make amends than it first may seem. Be creative. Make it fun. You may come up with a wild idea, but if it seems right to you, try it.

3. **Forgive yourself for all the "bad" things you've done.** This should be fairly easy since you've already taken responsibility for your past and present action. But to finish the job, you need to forgive yourself. To forgive yourself simply means to give up resentment against yourself, or give up the desire to punish yourself. Since you

have taken and are taking responsibility for your actions, to continue to punish yourself or resent yourself is just silly. You are human. Humans make mistakes. You've recognized that and corrected your mistakes. That's something to feel good about. So forgive yourself. A decision is all that's required. Simply decide to stop resenting yourself and give up any intentions of punishing yourself.

TAKE THESE THREE steps to a self you really like. You'll gain strength and confidence and the peace that comes from knowing you do what's right.

Fortify your integrity.

A good conscience is a continual Christmas.
— Benjamin Franklin

But there is a very tangible and very present Hell-on-this-earth which science has not yet helped us understand very well...it is this Hell— the Hell of neurosis and psychosis—to which sin and unexpiated guilt lead us.
— Dr. O.H. Mowrer

Rx to Relax

WHEN YOU GET ANGRY, upset, anxious, tense, frustrated, or worried, adrenaline goes into your blood stream. It makes your heart beat faster, putting strain on your cardiovascular system. These strains add up, and later in life, things can go wrong because of it. Every time you are able to lessen the intensity of one of these feelings, it will benefit your health. It also makes life a more pleasant experience.

There's a very simple way to lower your adrenaline level: Relax. Here's how to relax on the spot:

1. **Breathe deeply**. When you tense up, your breathing gets quicker, more shallow, and higher in the chest. You'll feel better right away, and your heart will slow down, if you'll just make

your breathing more relaxed. Deeper. Slower. Sigh in a relaxed way.

2. **Loosen tensed muscles**. Just about any time, but especially when you've got the adrenaline pumping, muscles tend to tighten, particularly muscles around your neck, upper back, and face. Pay attention to your muscles in those areas and when you find one that's contracting for no good reason, relax it. If at first you have trouble relaxing a muscle, tense it first, then relax it.

3. **Say the word "relax" to yourself**. Make sure your inner voice is relaxing. Don't yell at yourself, "Relax!!" Say it soothingly.

THESE THREE TASKS are easy to do, can be done in the midst of your work, and will slow your heart down to a healthier level. When you become more relaxed, you think better, you're more creative, and you can use more of what you know—including what you know about human relations, so you'll get along with people better. Your life will be smoother and better.

This is one of those little habits many people have formed that serves them well throughout their lives. I hope you use it too.

Breathe deeply, loosen tensed muscles, and say to yourself, "Relax."

Interest is Life

PEOPLE WHO ARE FULLY VITAL and alive and full of energy are *interested*. They're pursuing an interest. The stronger the interest, the more vitality emanates from it. People without any interests at all are bored, tired and lifeless. Interest is everything.

Here's the problem: You can't fake or force yourself to be interested in something. You can gently open yourself to be mildly interested, but you're either strongly interested in something or you're not, and it's not up to you. It's either there or it isn't.

There are subjects and activities which, if you pursued one of them, would awaken your sleeping vitality. But you may be ignoring them for "good reasons."

A woman I know liked to draw and was very good at it while she was still only in kindergarten. When she told her father she wanted to be an artist when she grew up, he said, "You don't want to be an artist. Artists don't make any money." He dismissed the idea with so much certainty, she dropped her interest immediately. She cut it off, turned away from it.

Many of us have had a similar experience. We turned away from what really interested us and now we don't really know what interests us. We look around at our options and don't see anything interesting because the thing that interests us is *behind* us, so to speak—we've turned out backs on it and can't see it any more.

I know a man who liked to sail as a youngster, but let it fade out of his life when he became an adult. He thought about it once in a while but figured he would do some sailing "later" when he had a lot of money and extra time (dream on dude). He recently decided to take up sailing, even on a small scale, and he has come alive.

Boredom is death. Interest is life. Dig up that dormant interest. You know the one—you've dropped it or laid it aside for perfectly sound reasons. You might even feel it's childish to pursue it. That's the one. Pursue it, even a little, and your awakened interest will brighten your whole life.

Pursue the interests that make you come alive.

Positive Thinking: The Next Generation

MAKING POSITIVE STATEMENTS TO YOURSELF when you feel down improves your mood—but only slightly. Thirty years ago, that was the best you could hope for. But since then, an enormous amount of research has been done on exactly how our thoughts affect the way we feel. This is the realm of cognitive science.

The most important insight from cognitive research is this: *When you feel angry, anxious, or depressed, those feelings are largely caused by irrational (unreasonable) assumptions.*

Of course, circumstances call for some kind of response, but your response will depend on your *habits of thinking.* When you're in the habit of making faulty (irrational, unreasonable, unjustifiable) assumptions in response to certain kinds of events, you're likely to feel a lot of anger, anxiety or sadness in that area of your life.

Cognitive science says, "Rather than trying to think positively, find out what's wrong with your negative thinking. If you've got strong negative feelings, your thinking is inevitably distorted, unsubstantiated and overgeneralized." Criticizing the assumptions behind your negative feelings measurably and significantly improves your mood. When you find yourself making an unreasonable assumption and it makes you feel bad, attack the assumption. Check it for illogic. See if you're exaggerating or ignoring evidence.

Give your own negative thoughts the same treatment you would give to the statements of a fast-talking salesman: Question them without mercy. Don't assume that something is true simply because *you* thought it. Check your own thoughts against logic and evidence as skeptically as you would the thoughts of someone else. You are fallible like any other human being, and you are capable of thinking thoughts that are not only untrue, but also counterproductive.

If you've got the time, criticize your assumptions *on paper*. Write an assumption you're making—something you think is true about the situation, some assessment or opinion you have—and then write out all the reasons why that assumption may not, in fact, be true, and why it may be a supremely stupid thing to think. This is one of my favorite methods. When I do this, I often use two pens of different color, one for the assumptions and one for my criticisms of those assumptions.

Old-style positive thinking—the kind of pollyanna, rose-colored glasses, everything-happens-for-a-reason positive thinking—ignores an important issue: truth. And that's why it doesn't work very well. Thinking positively only works if you *believe* it, and it's very difficult for a modern, educated, rational person (you, for instance) to believe something just because it's a nice thought.

Don't bother with positive thinking. Something much better has been discovered. When you feel mad, annoyed, frustrated, stressed, worried, or down-in-the-dumps, pay attention to your thoughts and then argue with those thoughts on the basis of evidence and reason. At the moment you recognize one of your negative thoughts as irrational, you'll feel better.

You may have to argue with the same thoughts over and over again, sometimes for months, but eventually you'll get in the habit of making more rational assumptions, and the more rational your thoughts, the less you'll be troubled by the negative emotions your thoughts were causing. When you're no longer burdened by unnecessary feelings of sadness, anger, and fear, you'll find your general mood and sense of well-being will rise to a new level. Cut yourself free of needless negative emotions with the blade of rationality.

Criticize the assumptions behind your negative feelings.

From Hope to Change

ACCORDING TO THE International Listening Association, within twenty-four hours, we forget half of any information we've heard. Forty-eight hours later, we've forgotten 75 percent of it. And we don't grasp everything we hear in the first place. But these numbers change when what we hear is *repeated*. And the more it's repeated, the better the numbers look.

All this has a huge bearing on how you make changes in your life. You change your behavior by changing the way you think. But the way you think is as ingrained and habitual and as resistant to change as any physical habit.

So learning new ways of thinking and behaving—and learning them well enough to actually make a difference—requires repetition. If, for example, you find a book that really makes a difference to you, read it again and again. Make it an annual event. Every time you read it, you'll come across things you'd forgotten about.

Audiotapes are ideal for repetition. Listen to tapes in your car and traffic jams will be transformed from an annoyance to an extended opportunity to improve the quality of your life.

Telling your friends about something you've learned helps cement the new information in your mind. The more you share it, the better you learn it. The effort and concentration it requires to explain something to someone makes it clearer in your own mind and more permanent.

There are always so many new books, new tapes, new shows, new ideas, new information—we know we'll never get to it all, but our curiosity constantly pulls us toward it. But keep this in mind: Most of that new stuff isn't very good. And even less applies to your situation. So when you come across something that *is* good and *does* apply to your situation, hold onto it. Reread it. When you come across a good chapter in this book that applies to you, read it again in a month. Write a letter to someone and explain the idea to them and how you used it and how it worked. Post it on your refrigerator. Read it onto a tape and listen to it in your car. Keep it in your life. Repetition makes a difference.

With repetition you can take a fleeting hope sparked by a good idea and turn it into an actual change in your life. Instead of that possibility fading with your memory, it can grow stronger and stronger until your life is changed for the better. The distance between hope and actuality is crossed by repetition.

To turn good ideas into real change, use repetition.

[What we] at first put on with some violence to natural inclination... [becomes] at length so easy...
— *Benjamin Franklin*

We are what we repeatedly do. Excellence, then, is not an act but a habit.
— *Aristotle*

[Calling something "natural"] does not mean it is beneficial or unchangeable. It is also natural to defecate in our pants, yet we teach ourselves to do the unnatural until the unnatural becomes second nature. Indeed, all self-discipline might be defined as teaching ourselves to do the unnatural.
— *M. Scott Peck*

Be All You Can Be

YOU USE ONLY 10 PERCENT of your brain. Have you ever heard that? It's nonsense. You and I use our whole brains. Ask any neurologist. There are no idle parts of the brain, no brain cells sitting around unused. For example, there are neurons in your brain stem whose job is to immobilize your body while you're dreaming so you don't physically act out your dreams and get up and run into a wall. Every part has its function.

Idiot-savants can be a genius at one thing, like mathematical calculations or music, but they pay for it with a corresponding deficit in other useful attributes, like getting along with others. What happens is that one function, like mathematical ability, takes over a larger percentage of brain tissue—commandeers it, so to speak, usually as a result of a brain injury at birth—but whatever other ability that part of the brain is normally used for goes wanting. What you often get are geniuses that can't have a decent relationship or tie their shoes or control their emotions.

All those abilities require brain space, and there's just barely enough with none to spare. Nature did not equip us with a bunch of extra brain cells. As it is, the brain is as big as it can get and still (barely) make it through the birth canal. If it were any bigger, normal births would be impossible.

You *could* learn more, do more, be more, for sure. But there is always a trade-off. You could use every spare moment, for example, listening to language tapes, and thereby learn ten more languages in your lifetime. But it would have consequences. You'd have less time to socialize, for one. And that would have other, possibly negative, consequences.

You *could* work all the time, always improving yourself at every moment of the day, but no play makes Johnny a dull boy. It's a trade-off. Balance is the key.

So don't feel bad that you're not "maximizing your full potential." Devote some time to your betterment, but also relax and enjoy the ride. You're alive on the planet, breathing air and capable of communicating with other fellow travelers. Enjoy it.

Improve yourself, but also relax and enjoy the ride.

Riches

IN AN EXPERIMENT at the University of Georgia, students were asked to remember a pleasant outdoor experience they'd had recently. Afterwards, they filled out a questionnaire rating their feelings of tension, relaxation and alertness.

Later the students experienced meditation by listening to recorded instructions with their eyes closed. Again, afterwards they filled out the questionnaire.

The verdict? Recalling a pleasant memory improved their concentration and lessened their anxiety *better* than meditation!

And recalling pleasant memories *strengthens those memories*. It makes those memories more real and easier to recall. Every event you experience in your life makes a pathway in your brain—a pattern of connections between neurons. But the pathway is weak. If you never recall that event again, your memory of it becomes weaker as time goes on until it becomes almost impossible to remember what happened, even if the experience was emotionally significant.

Some people are unhappy only because they don't remember the good times. Researchers find that depressed people have as many nice experiences as everyone else, but they don't *remember* them as well. They've gotten into the habit of reminiscing about the negative experiences, so *those* seem numerous and vivid, and they let all the positive experiences fade into the past. So it seems to them that life is tragic and filled with loss and misery.

Make it a point to recall your good times. Think about them now and then. Reminisce with your spouse or a friend or one of your children. Reminisce in letters to friends and relatives. They want to hear about your good times, anyway—especially recent good times—so let yourself go. Writing about them will strengthen your memories. When you look back on your life, it'll be easier to see the beauty of it, and your life in the present will feel richer.

Think back over the last couple of weeks and try to recall the small pleasures: the tiny victories, the little moments of kindness and love, the gentle feelings of satisfaction. Feel free to recall the big ones too, but you have a lot more small ones, and you'll probably be surprised to realize how many you have.

Reminisce about special times of your life: moments of love, of awakening, of turning points, of great insight. Remember the events that help give life meaning. Remember the times that have shaped your life, or that you *want* to shape your life. You have had special moments when you saw how wonderful life could be or when you gained some unusual insight. If nothing more is done with those, the memory of them and the power of the insights can fade. Remember those moments. Remember what they meant. Remember what they *could* mean and your memory will help make it so.

Reminisce about the good times and the special times. Strengthen those memories. Store them up. They are your true riches.

Reminisce about the best times.

*I wept as I remembered
how often you and I
Had tired the sun with talking
and sent him down the sky.*

— *Callimachus*

*To look backward for a while is to
refresh the eye, to restore it, and
to render it the more fit for its
prime function of looking forward.*

— *Margaret Fairless Barber*

Adventure

IN HIS MEMOIR, *Education of a Wandering Man*, Louis L'Amour wrote, "As I have said elsewhere, and more than once, I believe adventure is nothing but a romantic word for trouble....What people speak of as adventure is something nobody in his right mind would seek out, and it becomes romantic only when one is safely at home."

If adventure is only a romantic word for trouble, then it follows that *you can see trouble as an adventure*. In other words, trouble isn't a reality; it's a judgement. And "adventure" would be an equally valid judgement.

I was once in an argument with my wife, for example, that was getting too heated, so I took a break, went down to the library to calm down, and thought about what

L'Amour said. And I asked myself, "How is this fight like an adventure?"

"Well," I replied to myself, "I'm doing something I don't do very often—hanging out at the library. And doing something I don't normally do must be one of the prerequisites for an experience I can call an adventure."

Musing over this question, I thought, "The fight itself is like a jungle. Can we find our way through it to the River of Love? I think so. But we may get temporarily lost in the tangled valley of Being Right. We may sink in the quicksand of Hurt Feelings. We may miss the shortcut of Forgiveness and have to take the long way around.

"There are predators to look out for: We can get eaten alive by Dredging Up Past Injustices. The Unwillingness to Exercise Self-Control is somewhat like a swarm of mosquitoes that can inject us with malaria and make us sick for a long time, slowing down our progress through the jungle.

"We must somehow get across the chasm of our differences. One of us can cross it alone or we can meet half way."

And after thinking about it this way, I went home and talked to Klassy with a different attitude. A better attitude. Try it. When you run into trouble, ask yourself: "How is this like an adventure?"

Ask yourself, "How is this like an adventure?"

The Ocelot Blues

WHAT HAPPENS WHEN YOU let your mind wander? Studies have shown when a human mind has nothing specific to think about, it becomes chaotic, flitting from one thought to another in a random way. But if any mind— your mind, my mind—keeps wandering, before long, our thoughts will land on something that grabs our attention: some fear or frustration or unfinished business. You know what this is like: Your mind sticks there, like a tire spinning in the mud, dwelling on the worrisome or upsetting thought, and it ruins your mood. This is what happens to a mind without a purpose.

Having a purpose on your mind keeps your thoughts from devolving into chaos and bad moods. You can't stop your mind from thinking, but when you have a goal to think about, your mental resources are less likely to drift randomly into upsetting thoughts. They have someplace to go.

That's why studies show that people are more often in a good mood while working than they are in their free time. It seems unbelievable at first, but it is easily explained by the need for purpose. Most people are more likely to have clear purposes at work than at home.

It is common knowledge that "idle hands are the devil's workshop," but the important factor, the factor that gets you out of the devil's workshop, is *something you need to do* that compels your attention.

Remember that: Something you need to do that compels your attention. That's the key—think of it as vitamin P.

The human mind *needs* a purpose. It's like the ocelot scratching off his fur at the Seattle Zoo. The zookeepers didn't know what to do about it. They gave him a female, but he kept skinning himself. They changed his diet. They changed his cage. But he kept clawing at himself.

Finally, someone realized that in the wild, ocelots eat birds. So instead of giving the ocelot meat to eat, they threw an unplucked chicken into the cage. Sure enough, the ocelot—using the same clawing movements he was using on himself—plucked the feathers out of that chicken and stopped skinning himself.

Your mind is like that. It needs a bone to chew or it'll chew the furniture. It needs a purpose. And not just any purpose, but something that challenges you, engages you, something you intend to accomplish, something you *want*, something real and concrete. Your mind aligns around that goal instead of being pulled into negativity, and you're happier.

**Find a purpose that enthralls you
and then actively pursue it.**

---

*Without commitment, life is
nothing but a long wait.*

— *Steven Forrest*

*One of the most dangerous forms of
human error is forgetting what one
is trying to achieve.*

— *Paul Nitze*

*The only true happiness comes from
squandering ourselves for a purpose.*

— *William Cowper*

Argue With Yourself —and Win!

WHEN SOMEONE MAKES YOU ANGRY, it may seem that the cause of your anger is the other person's actions. But what really makes you angry is what you *think* the action *means*. If you look closely at the meaning of an event, your certainty about it will fade. You'll realize it doesn't necessarily mean what you think it means. This uncertainty will make your anger diminish.

Suppose, for example, someone interrupts you while you're talking and it makes you mad. You "know" the person is being disrespectful. On closer look, you see that: 1) an event happens, 2) you figure out what it means, and then, 3) you feel an emotion in response to the meaning you created.

Step number two happens very fast—so fast it seems the event directly caused your feelings. But that isn't so. And you can prove it to yourself.

Wait until the next time you get mad at someone. Then try to discover one thought you have about what they did. You may have to backtrack—do a slow-motion replay. Ask yourself, "Why am I mad?" Your answer is probably, "Because he did such-and-such." Ask yourself another question: "Why would *that* make me angry?" Your answer to this second question is probably a statement about the *meaning* of the action. Now you have something to work with.

Take your statement and look at it scientifically. In the above example, someone interrupted you. You thought, "He doesn't respect me." Looking at that thought scientifically, you realize it's a theory to explain why he interrupted you. Once you look at it, you also realize *it isn't the only explanation possible*! Try to come up with other explanations: "Maybe he never thought much about interrupting, and no one ever said anything to him about it, so he's in the habit of interrupting people—those he respects and those he doesn't." Or "Maybe he interrupted me because he has a poor memory and didn't want to forget his thought, so he blurted it out." You can never really be sure why another person does something. Sometimes the person himself doesn't know why he's doing it.

After you create two or three good theories (this will only take a few moments), your anger will fade, you'll feel better, and you'll deal with the situation more rationally. Argue with yourself this way and everyone wins!

When you're angry, argue with *yourself* first.

---

*People who fly into a rage always
make a bad landing.*

— Will Rogers

*You will not be punished FOR your anger.
You will be punished BY your anger.*

— Buddha

*To accuse neither oneself nor others shows
that one's education is complete.*

— Epictetus

*While you're saving your face,
you're losing your ass.*

— Lyndon B. Johnson

Constitutional Right

"ABOVE ALL," wrote the Danish philosopher Søren Kierkegaard, "do not lose your desire to walk. Every day I walk myself into a state of well-being and walk away from every illness. I have walked myself into my best thoughts...."

Friedrich Nietzsche, the German philosopher, went so far as to say "All truly great thoughts are conceived while walking."

A walk taken regularly for the sake of one's well-being is called a *constitutional*. Kierkegaard and Nietzsche were in good company. Gandhi, Darwin, Emerson, and many creative (and long-lived) people throughout history took constitutionals often. You can too. Here's how to have a good one:

1. **Walk at a pace that's easy and pleasant**. Don't make your constitutionals do double duty as an exercise program. A constitutional is closer to meditation, but it's not a "discipline." It's more like a vacation, and that's exactly the attitude to have.

2. **Bring a little pocket-sized notebook and a pen**, but don't try to get ideas. Of course, you'll sometimes think of things you want to remember. Taking notes is a way to free your mind— once your idea is down on paper, you're free to forget about it for the moment.

3. **Walk for longer than fifteen minutes**. A half hour to an hour is good. You need to do it long enough to let your mind relax. This is a temporary vacation from our compulsion to *do*, and it needs to be long enough to have an effect.

ON A WALK, you get a fresh perspective; you can find solutions to problems; you look at things more clearly. You become calmer, saner and healthier. It's easier to think because, 1) you have the *time* to think, 2) there's nothing else you need to attend to, and 3) your brain is getting more oxygen.

This way of taking a walk is aptly named: It's good for your *constitution*—your overall well-being, body and mind. You have a *right* to some quiet time to yourself, so exercise your right. A haven of peace and sanity awaits you...only a few steps away.

**Clear your head and relax
by going for a long walk.**

It is a peculiarity of humor in me, my strong propensity for strolling. I deliberately shut up my books...put on my old clothes and old hat, and slip with the greatest satisfaction into a little cow-path, where I am sure I can defy observation.

— Ralph Waldo Emerson

The turbulent billows of the fretful surface leave the deep parts of the ocean undisturbed; and to him who has a hold on vaster and more permanent realities, the hourly vicissitudes of his personal destiny seem relatively insignificant things.

— William James

Why Ask Why?

A QUESTION THAT NATURALLY comes to mind when something goes wrong is "Why?" But it's a question fraught with danger. Research has repeatedly shown that the human brain is designed to answer a question with whatever knowledge it has (no matter how little) and come up with a plausible answer (however wrong). Self-blame or victimhood is a frequent side effect.

For example, you can ask why you're overweight and, without any problem at all, your mind will come up with answers. But all it can give you are theories. What's the "real" answer? Is it because you weren't loved as a child? Is it a genetic weakness in your family? Is it an evolutionary holdover precaution against famine? Is your mouth simply bored?

The problem with a WHY question is that you get too many answers you can do nothing about. You can't change your childhood or a genetic weakness.

There is only one good thing about asking WHY: It can be entertaining. It's intriguing. It's like a mystery and mysteries capture our attention like nothing else. But if what you want is to handle the situation well or solve the problem and get on with the business of living, ask HOW not WHY. It's more efficient.

Since your mind will try to answer any question you put to it, the kind of question you ask makes a *big* difference. So ask what you really want to know: "How could I get slimmer?" Or "How can I avoid this problem in the future?" Or "How can I solve this problem now?" Or "How can I make things a little better?" Let your mind go wild on one of those questions. The answers will be more productive.

With HOW, you go straight for a useful answer. You avoid getting sidetracked into what can become an endless search for "understanding." With HOW your answers lead to actions. And it is actions that solve problems and produce real change.

Instead of asking why you have a problem, ask how you can get what you want.

Science of Happiness

HAPPY PEOPLE HAVE SOMETHING IN COMMON. It's not money and it's not fame. According to researchers David G. Myers, professor of psychology at Hope College, and Ed Diener, professor or psychology at the University of Illinois, happy people are healthier and share the following four traits:

1. They like themselves.
2. They have a high degree of personal control.
3. They are optimistic.
4. They are extroverts.

THE GOOD NEWS is that *none of these are fixed*—each can be cultivated. If you are weak in any of these four traits, you can become happier by strengthening it.

1. **Like yourself more by doing better.** Improve your ethics—when you stop fudging on something, you stop beating yourself up for fudging. Increase your ability—when you are more skilled at something, you admire yourself more, both for your new ability and for the perseverance it took to attain it. Treat people better—because we're social animals, when we help others like *themselves* more, it comes around and helps us like *ourselves* more too.

2. **Gain more control of your time by directly seeking it**. This includes reading time-management books and applying what you learn. But keep this in mind: No matter how good you are, if you keep increasing the number of pans in the fire, at some point you'll start to lose control. Decrease the number of pans until you have good control. With practice you may be able to increase that number. But maintain control in the meantime.

3. **Be more optimistic by studying Martin Seligman's work** and the ATTITUDE section of this book. In his book *Learned Optimism*, Seligman outlines the three key areas where a change

will make a difference and shows you exactly
how to make those changes.

**4. Become more extroverted by studying and
practicing the classic *How to Win Friends and
Influence People* by Dale Carnegie** and the
PEOPLE section of this book. It helps to begin
with the supposition that introversion is simply
a lack of ability to deal with people. Then,
remedy that lack. Carnegie's book is still on the
bookshelves after all these years because it's the
best collection of information about how to deal
with people that has ever been written.

NO MATTER HOW happy or unhappy you are now, you
can make your life a happier one, and you can do it one
small step at a time.

To become happier:
**Strengthen your integrity, get better control
of your time, become more optimistic,
and practice good human relations.**

---

*Assume the virtue, even if you have it not
For use almost can change
the stamp of nature.*

— *William Shakespeare*

A Slave to His Destiny

ONE MORNING A SIXTEEN-YEAR-OLD BOY was kidnapped from his house by a band of knife-wielding thugs and taken to another country, there to be sold as a slave. The year was 401 A.D.

He was made a shepherd. Slaves were not allowed to wear clothes, so he was often dangerously cold and frequently on the verge of starvation. He spent months at a time without seeing another human being—a severe psychological torture.

But this greatest of difficulties was transformed into the greatest of blessings because it gave him an opportunity not many get in a lifetime. Long lengths of solitude have been used by people all through history to meditate, to learn to control the mind and to explore the depths of feeling and thought to a degree impossible in the hubbub of normal life.

He wasn't looking for such an "opportunity," but he got it anyway. He had never been a religious person, but to hold himself together and take his mind off the pain, he began to pray, so much that "...in one day," he wrote later, "I would say as many as a hundred prayers and after dark nearly as many again...I would wake and pray before daybreak—through snow, frost, and rain...."

This young man, at the onset of his manhood, got a "raw deal." But therein lies the lesson. Nobody gets a perfect life. The question is *not* "What could I have done if I'd gotten a better life?" but rather "What can I do with the life I've got?"

How can you take *your* personality, *your* circumstances, *your* upbringing, the time and place *you* live in, and make something extraordinary out of it? What *can* you do with what you've got?

The young slave prayed. He didn't have much else available to do, so he did what he could with all his might. And after six years of praying, he heard a voice in his sleep say that his prayers would be answered: He was going home. He sat bolt upright and the voice said, "Look, your ship is ready."

He was a long way from the ocean, but he started walking. After two hundred miles, he came to the ocean and there was a ship, preparing to leave for Britain, his homeland. Somehow he got aboard the ship and went home to reunite with his family.

But he had changed. The sixteen-year-old boy had become a holy man. He had visions. He heard the voices of the people from the island he had left—Ireland—calling him back. The voices were persistent, and he eventually left his family to become ordained as a priest and a bishop with the intention of returning to Ireland and converting the Irish to Christianity.

At the time, the Irish were fierce, illiterate, Iron-Age people. For over eleven hundred years, the Roman Empire had been spreading its civilizing influence from Africa to Britain, but Rome never conquered Ireland.

The people of Ireland warred constantly. They made human sacrifices of prisoners of war and sacrificed newborns to the gods of the harvest. They hung the skulls of their enemies on their belts as ornaments.

Our slave-boy-turned-bishop decided to make these people literate and peaceful. Braving dangers and obstacles of tremendous magnitude, he actually *succeeded!* By the end of his life, Ireland was Christian. Slavery had ceased entirely. Wars were much less frequent, and literacy was spreading.

How did he do it? He began by teaching people to read—starting with the Bible. Students eventually became teachers and went to other parts of the island to create new places of learning, and wherever they went, they brought the know-how to turn sheepskin into paper and paper into books.

Copying books became the major religious activity of that country. The Irish had a long-standing love of words, and it expressed itself to the full when they became literate. Monks spent their lives copying books: the Bible, the lives of saints, and the works accumulated by the Roman culture—Latin, Greek, and Hebrew books, grammars, the works of Plato, Aristotle, Virgil, Homer, Greek philosophy, math, geometry, astronomy.

In fact, because so many books were being copied, they were saved, because as Ireland was being civilized, the Roman Empire was falling apart. Libraries disappeared in Europe. Books were no longer copied (except in the city of Rome itself), and children were no longer taught to read. The civilization that had been built up over eleven centuries disintegrated. This was the beginning of the Dark Ages.

Because our slave-boy-turned-bishop transformed his suffering into a mission, civilization itself, in the form of literature and the accumulated knowledge contained in that literature, was saved and not lost during that time of darkness. He was named a saint, the famous Saint Patrick. You can read the full and fascinating story if you like in the excellent book *How the Irish Saved Civilization* by Thomas Cahill.

"Very interesting," you might say, "but what does that have to do with me?"

Well...you are also in some circumstances or other, and it's not all peaches and cream, is it? There's some stuff you don't like—maybe something about your circumstances, perhaps, or maybe some events that occurred in your childhood.

But here you are, with *that* past, with *these* circumstances, with the things you consider less than ideal. What are you going to do with them? If those circumstances have made you uniquely qualified for some contribution, what would it be?

You may not know the answer to that question right now, but keep in mind that the circumstances you think only spell misery may contain the seeds of something profoundly Good. Assume that's true, and the assumption will begin to gather evidence until your misery is transformed, as Saint Patrick's suffering was, from a raw deal to the perfect preparation for something better.

Ask yourself and keep asking, "Given my upbringing and circumstances, what Good am I especially qualified to do?"

---

*An aim is the only fortune worth finding;
and it is not to be found in foreign lands
but in the heart itself.*

— *Robert Louis Stevenson*

*Every human being is intended to have a
character of his own; to be what no other is,
and to do what no other can do.*

— *William Channing*

Attitude Principles

When bad happens:
Assume it won't last long, look to see what *isn't* affected, and don't indulge in self-blame.

When good happens:
Consider its effects permanent, see how much of your life is affected, and look to see how much you can take credit for.

Become more optimistic.

**Talk to yourself in a confident,
reassuring, positive way.**

Do some honest good in the world.

**Come up with alternative ways
of interpreting an event.**

Change the *details* of your thoughts.

Tell yourself you can handle it.

No matter what happens, assume it's good.

Keep persisting until the change you want happens.

**Describe upsetting situations to yourself
in emotionally neutral words.**

Control what is your responsibility.

**Direct your thoughts to what
you appreciate and say it.**

**If your own greed is making you discontent,
quit cramming so much into your days.**

**Direct your mind by asking yourself
a good question.**

**When something "bad" happens,
say to yourself, "That's good!"**

**Relieve negative feelings by turning your attention
to purposeful activities.**

Let go of an idea that causes you needless stress.

**Find a way to turn your problems
into an advantage.**

Interpret events in a way that helps you.

**Wonder about what *good* things
might be happening.**

Be skeptical of your feelings of certainty.

When you hit a setback in life:
**Assume the problem or its consequences
won't last long, see how you can prevent the same
problem in the future, and don't jump to the
conclusion that this setback will ruin everything.**

To improve your self-esteem:
**Gain more ability, become more honest,
do something worthwhile, and acknowledge people.**

Make up your mind you will succeed.

**Think thoughts that give you strength
and make you tough.**

Exercise regularly.

**Act as though you already feel
the way you *want* to feel.**

Remind yourself you don't need much to be happy.

Fortify your integrity.

**Breathe deeply, loosen tensed muscles,
and say to yourself, "Relax."**

Pursue the interests that make you come alive.

**Criticize the assumptions behind
your negative feelings.**

To turn good ideas into real change, use repetition.

Improve yourself, but also relax and enjoy the ride.

Reminisce about the best times.

Ask yourself, "How is this like an adventure?"

Find a purpose that enthralls you
and then actively pursue it.

When you're angry, argue with *yourself* first.

Clear your head and relax by going for a long walk.

Instead of asking why you have a problem,
ask how you can get what you want.

To become happier:
Strengthen your integrity, get better control
of your time, become more optimistic,
and practice good human relations.

Ask yourself and keep asking, "Given my
upbringing and circumstances, what Good
am I especially qualified to do?"

Work

Zoning Out

AT ONE EXTREME, work can be overwhelmingly stressful. At the other end of the spectrum, work can be completely boring. Somewhere in the middle, the work is challenging enough to compel your attention and yet not enough to completely outstrip your ability. When you hit that perfect middle zone, work becomes a pleasure.

Mihaly Csikszentmihalyi at the University of Chicago discovered that people reach this zone more often at work (54 percent of the time) than in leisure (18 percent of the time). When in this zone, people feel creative, active, concentrated, strong and happy—more so than when they're *not* in that zone.

Work has gotten a bad reputation, probably from the beginning of this century when working conditions were horrible. But those days are over and clearly we have the opportunity to experience a lot of satisfaction while working. *The key is matching our skill to the challenge confronting us.* When challenges and skills are well matched, we enter the zone. When they are *not* matched, it's unpleasant—too much challenge is stressful; not enough is boring.

If you are experiencing stress and tension at work, the solution is to *increase your skill* until it matches your challenge. For example, a typist buried in a backlog of unfinished work feels overwhelmed and tense. The feeling of tension tells him something: He has too much challenge. The solution is *more skill,* so he asks himself, "What skill could I improve to help me catch up on my backlog?" Maybe his answer is "Typing speed." He buys a typing-tutor program and practices after work. His typing speed increases (and his stress level decreases) until eventually his skill level matches the challenge of the job, and his work enters The Enjoyment Zone.

To cure boredom on the job, you go the other way: Increase the challenge. The way to increase the challenge is to set and pursue goals beyond what is required by the job. Get the job done well *and* attain some other targets simultaneously. Let's say our typist's program of self-improvement worked so well that it's now a year later and he no longer has any backlog. In fact, he's getting all his work done ahead of time! His job is no longer stressful. Now it's boring.

Boredom makes you feel tired and even apathetic. You feel like you need rest, but what you really need is more challenge.

There are hundreds of ways our typist could increase his challenge. I'll give you two. First, he could try to make his typing as perfect as possible: using the correct finger for every letter, never looking at the keyboard, making no spelling errors, etc. And then, keeping these high standards, he could try to continuously increase his speed. Second, he could look around and see what other challenges (related to the job) he could tackle—reorganizing, making systems more efficient, etc.

Now here's the catch. You knew there was a catch, didn't you? In the pursuit of The Enjoyment Zone, your skills keep increasing. So you need to keep increasing the challenge to keep up with it or you slip out of the zone and into boredom.

But keeping a good match between skills and challenges isn't as hard as it sounds, and the result is more enjoyment, so it's worth the trouble. And since increasing skills are usually associated with increased opportunities for promotions and raises, there is another possible side effect you might enjoy: More money.

If you're bored, increase your challenge.
If you're stressed, increase your skill.

Work banishes those three great evils:
boredom, vice and poverty.

— Voltaire

Time Management Made Simple

A LOT OF BOOKS have been written about how to manage your time by eliminating wasted motion and saving seconds where you can. But that's how you make a factory more efficient, not a human being.

People have one main source of inefficiency: We're prone to get sidetracked or distracted from the important things that need to be done and somewhat lost in the numerous unimportant things we also want to do. So the secret of becoming more efficient is first, *know what's important*, and second, *avoid getting off track*. These can both be accomplished with a single technique.

Of all the words written about time management, the most valuable technique can be stated in one sentence: MAKE A LIST AND PUT IT IN ORDER.

There are always things to do. Since none of us can hold much in our minds while busy doing other things, we need to write things down or we forget—or have the uneasy feeling that we might be forgetting. So you need to make a list.

Write down only the *important* things you need to do. This should be a *small* list, no more than six items. Don't clutter up your list with trivial or obvious things. This isn't a schedule book, it's a To Do List, and its purpose is to keep you focused.

You've made your list. Now, put the tasks in the order of their importance. Putting the list in order makes your decisions smooth and effective. You'll know what to do first (the most important), and you'll always know what to do next. You also know you're making the best use of your time because at any given moment you're doing the most important thing you need to do.

There's no need to rush around or feel stressed to be efficient. Feeling tense or pressured makes you *less* efficient in the long run by causing unnecessary conflicts with people, mistakes, illness, and burnout. You are in more control of your life when you are calm.

Make a list and put it in order. This puts your mind in order and puts your day in order. It's a good investment of your time because you'll get more done that really matters.

Make a list and put it in order.

Envision It Done

HERE'S A RULE we all know we ought to follow: Do the important things first. You and I know if we're doing something of secondary importance while we still have something of primary importance to do, we're essentially wasting our time—even if what we're doing is constructive, productive, positive, loving, or any other worthwhile description. If it isn't one of the few things that are important to us, then it's a waste of time.

Of course that's a rather extreme and absolute thing to say, and there are always mitigating circumstances and perfectly valid reasons why the rule can't be followed all the time, but doing important things first is a rule few would argue with.

Important tasks are usually more difficult than unimportant tasks, so we tend to put them off. But listen: That's because we're thinking about what it will be like to *do* the task. And that's where we go wrong. Don't think about that. Think about what it will be like to have the task *done.* There's a big difference—a difference that can make a difference. It takes your attention off the part you don't like and puts your focus on something you really want: the result. That subtle difference will make the task more appealing, so you'll be less likely to put it off.

Instead of looking at the bills to be paid and thinking about all the time and frustration and neck-hurting hassle, imagine the feeling you'll get when you finish, when all the bills are stacked up there, paid, stamped and ready to mail. What a great feeling! Keep that image in mind when you look at the stack of bills. You'll get to it sooner.

And when you get to something sooner, you suffer less because you spend less psychological effort avoiding the task. You get to spend more of your time on the other side—satisfied that the job is finished.

That's it. It's a simple change that makes things better. Vividly anticipate the *completion* of important tasks and you will get more of them done.

**Vividly imagine the *completion*
of important tasks.**

Use What You Get

I WAS AT A PUBLICITY SEMINAR recently and the speaker said something very useful. She suggested that when you do a TV interview, you decide beforehand what message you want to communicate to the viewers, and then, *no matter what the interviewer asks you*, make sure you answer with your message.

Of course you have to acknowledge the question somehow and make the transition to your answer smooth, but, she said, no matter what, you must stay on what you want to say and not get sidetracked by the interviewer.

She was an expert in her field and said this was good advice. Some interviewers are downright hostile. Even if they aren't, they often have a different purpose than you do for being there. So the question becomes: "Whose goal will be achieved? Yours or theirs?" Of course, if your two intentions are not wholly antagonistic, it is possible that both of you can be satisfied.

The same principle operates not only on TV interviews, but in regular life too. The first and most important principle is to know what you want. *Know what you want.* It doesn't mean you have to step all over everyone to get it. But your wishes are at least as valid as anyone else's, and from your perspective they are *more* valid than anyone else's. That's the way it ought to be.

So take whatever you get from the world—your circumstances, the people in your life and what they're trying to accomplish—and use it to accomplish your goals.

To do this you have to focus on what you intend to accomplish, and go after it like a hungry lion stalking her prey. No matter what happens, keep trying to accomplish your purpose. It takes some concentration and a little practice. But you'll be able to achieve your goals with more certainty. And you won't be drained as much by things unrelated to your purpose.

Your goals are honorable and valuable. Don't let them get shunted aside by pushy people or less-than-ideal circumstances. Take whatever the world presents to you and use it to accomplish your purpose. No matter what.

**Whatever happens, use it
to accomplish your purpose.**

Do You Want to Give Up?

WE HAVE GOALS—things we want to accomplish. And we really *do* want to accomplish them; we're not trying to fool anyone or pump things up. But sometimes we give up on our goals. Why?

All goals have obstacles to their achievement, things in the way. These are problems or difficulties we meet on the way to the goal that we *must* handle in order to achieve the goal.

What makes us give up is when it looks like we won't be able to overcome the obstacles. They seem too big or too numerous. When we feel *sure* we can't do it, we tend to give up.

What are the alternatives to giving up? Below are three. They are stated simply. Please do not discount them because of their brevity or simplicity. The fact that they are stated simply and briefly merely makes them easier to use and therefore *more* powerful, not less.

Get help. There are people who want to help you. Enlist their aid. The more help you get, the sooner you'll succeed.

Tackle the obstacles one at a time. When you try to tackle all the obstacles, or just *look* at all the obstacles at the same time, it can overwhelm you. The feeling of being completely outgunned can take the wind out of your sails before you even get started. Pick one obstacle—an easy one—and tackle that first. Don't even think about the rest of them. It's likely that after you've tackled one obstacle, you'll be in a better, stronger position to handle the next one, and so on.

Get some training or knowledge that will make you more able to deal with the obstacles. Read, study, practice. As you gain in ability, the obstacles shrink in comparison.

NEXT TIME YOU are overwhelmed by obstacles, try one, two, or all three of these alternatives to giving up. You'll find they work. Using them, you'll discover new strength and zeal to keep your dream alive and accomplish your goal.

Rather than give up:
Get help, tackle the obstacles one at a time, and get some training.

Those who dream by night in the dusty recesses of their minds wake in the day to find that all was vanity; but the dreamers of the day are dangerous men, for they may act their dream with open eyes and make it possible.

— T.E. Lawrence

Whatsoever thy hand findeth to do, do it with thy might; for there is no work, nor device, nor knowledge, nor wisdom in the grave, whither thou goest.

— Ecclesiastes

As Good As Gold

ONE FUNDAMENTAL FORCE allows you to make changes in your life and turn good ideas into reality. The greatest idea, the finest resolution, the best plan are all useless without it.

What is this fundamental force? It is the power of keeping your word. It's the attitude of honoring the promises you make as *sacred*—even (or maybe especially) the promises you make to yourself.

The good news is you can increase your ability to keep your word. You can make this power more available to yourself.

First, understand the fundamental role it plays. Recognize its power.

Next, don't commit yourself lightly—treat each promise you make as something you *will* do no matter what. Be very selective about what you commit yourself to.

And finally, renew your commitment every time you break your word.

Each of us has what Abraham Maslow called "choice-points" every day. These are moments when we have to decide, "Am I going to do the thing I promised myself and move forward? Or am I going to do the easy thing and break my promise and move backward?"

And if you break your promise, you arrive at another choice-point: Will you renew your commitment to be a person who keeps your word? Or will you give up on yourself and adjust your self-image downward? The decisions you make during these choice-points determine the direction and quality of your life.

The most important starting point is to make a promise to yourself that, from this day forward, when you come to a choice-point, you will choose to keep your word. The more often you make the choice to keep your word, the more your word is worth. Eventually, your word is as good as gold.

Keep your word.

Law of Return

ON MY PAGE-A-DAY CALENDAR, I read this: "Render more and better service than that for which you are paid and sooner or later you'll receive compound interest on compound interest from your investment."

Of course it's ridiculous to believe there is *actually* compound interest accumulating somewhere in the ether, but it is extremely useful to *think* of your effort in that way because that thought can make itself true.

When you think that way, you will work hard and enjoy it because you are assuming you'll be compensated for any work you do. Why not work hard? Any money you're not making right away for your extra effort is earning compound interest for you. Your extra effort is an investment that will be paid to you eventually. So your attitude is good and you are willing to work long and hard. And because you do, *you* will be the first one to be promoted. *You* will be the one the customer seeks out. *You* will be the one who is indispensable. People will notice the extra service and it will work in your favor constantly. Your original belief in this maxim becomes true by virtue of your belief in it.

And look at what happens to a person who *doesn't* think that way. Imagine a person who thinks, "I'm not going to put out any more work until they pay me more." Now if you were the boss, will this be the first person you consider for a promotion? If you were the customer, is that the person you want to do business with? No! Not if there is someone down the road who is giving more and better service than you pay her for. She will get the business. She will get the promotion. She is more of a pleasure to work with. Her rewards may not be immediate, but they will come. It's the Law of Return.

It is only human nature to want to do business with someone who is trying hard and has a good attitude. It's human nature to promote someone like that. They're obviously an asset. Many *many* people just try to get by. So when you work to accumulate "compound interest," you stand out...and your ship comes in.

Assume extra effort is an investment that returns to you with compound interest.

Personality Counts

A PLEASANT PERSONALITY is important for salespeople and shopkeepers, but what about the rest of us? Isn't competence enough? Doesn't technical skill count more than anything?

A team of researchers at Purdue University wanted to find out. They studied the careers of a group of engineering graduates to find out if personality played any part in the engineer's level of success. After testing and follow-up, the researchers discovered that those who had the greatest mastery of the technical material made only slightly more money than the engineers with the least technical capability. But those who tested high in personality factors earned about 15 percent more than those with the high technical ability and about *33 percent* more than those who tested low in personality factors.

Engineering is a technical field. And even here, personality makes a big difference.

Of course, in truly perilous conditions, where lives depend on skill, personality doesn't matter much. Or does it? For Charles Houston and Robert Bates, the leaders of an expedition, the *most* important quality they sought was personality. The expedition in question was the fifth attempt to conquer K2, the second highest mountain in the world. They needed a team of eight experienced climbers. What did they look for? At the top of their list was "a good personality."

Houston and Bates had learned from previous expeditions that certain qualities of personality can prove essential to a group's survival. They knew from experience that if they were to succeed, each mountaineer on the team must "be able to keep his good nature and add to the humor of the party when bad weather, danger, or hardships strain the nerves." Even here, even in harsh survival conditions, the principle applies.

No matter what you do or where you are, your personality counts. When you try to get along better with others, when you exercise or eat better or get more sleep to improve your disposition, when you learn to handle stress or conflict or nervousness or depression a little better—it makes a difference. On an engineering team or at the top of a mountain or at the water cooler down the hall, it makes a difference. Personality counts.

Increase your ability to get along with people and improve your disposition.

Good character is more to be praised than outstanding talent. Most talents are, to some extent, a gift. Good character, by contrast, is not given to us. We have to build it piece by piece—by thought, choice, courage and determination.

— *John Luther*

We are here to do good to others. What the others are here for, I don't know.

— *W.H. Auden*

R-e-s-p-e-c-t

IT'S NICE TO BE LIKED, but it is even more satisfying to be respected. And although it takes some effort, you can attain that desire. Here are three places your effort will increase the respect you get from people:

> **Increase your competence**. People respect ability and skill, as long as you are noticeably good. This means trying to be a jack-of-all-trades doesn't work. Concentrate your efforts. Choose a useful ability and hone yourself into the Mozart of that ability. If the skill is used at your job, your increasing competence may bring you a new

pay level too. Work on improving your ability whenever you can. Become a master.

Use good manners. Without using *please* and *thank you* and *would you mind*, without saying *hi* to people and learning their names and interests, you will not earn people's respect. Even if you're competent, you will be resented rather than admired.

Speak up rather than smolder. Do it with good manners, but speak. It takes courage to speak up, and people know that and respect it. But when you speak up, make requests rather than simply complaining. Don't say what you don't like about what's already been done; say what you'd like to see in the future. And think it through beforehand so you say it well.

DON'T WORRY ABOUT whether or not people like you. Concentrate on competence and good manners and saying what you need to say, and you'll get more than liking. You'll get even more than respect from others. You'll earn the reward that might matter more than any other: You'll respect yourself.

To earn more respect:
Increase your competence, use good manners, and speak up rather than smolder.

A Terrible Thing to Waste

DO YOU SOMETIMES FEEL TIRED? Listless? It might be *boredom*. Some tasks are just plain boring, and when your mind is bored, it starts shutting down or drifting off and going to sleep. To stay awake, you must *engage your mind*. Here are a couple of ideas to help you:

> **Move faster**. This makes your mind pay closer attention in order to avoid mistakes. This demand for increased attention wakes you up, focuses your mind and makes the task more challenging. You can speed up without feeling unpleasantly stressed: Make it like a game. How much can

you get done in the next half hour? Set a target and see if you can reach it. This makes a tedious task less boring and, as a bonus, frees up more time for things you like to do.

Listen to something. Everyone knows it's more fun to do physical work while listening to good music than it is working in silence. Music engages your mind to some degree. But there is something that engages your mind more completely: talking. There has been a virtual explosion in the publishing industry of books and seminars on audiotape. Many people who commute to work have converted that boring and otherwise unproductive time into a mind-engaging education. The amount of material available on tape is staggering. In the next few years, using only the time you spend driving and doing household chores, you can learn a foreign language, listen to countless great books read to you by the best readers in America, and transform boring routines into an opportunity to expand your mind.

There's another kind of value to tapes. Often it doesn't matter what you *have* learned. Even if you could recite it, some practical knowledge matters only if you *have it in mind*. Ideas about human relations are like that. I have pretty much memorized the principles in Dale Carnegie's book *How to Win Friends and Influence People*, but when I am face-to-face with a real human being, I often forget it all. It isn't fresh in my mind—it's stored away somewhere. For this kind of knowledge, it's better to listen to a little every day. Then the ideas will be in the front of your mind when you need them.

USE THESE TWO ideas to make boring tasks more interesting to your mind. Move faster, listen to something, or both. A mind is truly a terrible thing to waste. Brains are made to be constantly interested. Brains aren't like muscles; muscles get tired when they are used too much. Brains get tired *when they aren't used enough*. Brains not only get tired, but over time, they can become smaller and more feeble.

Research is now showing that it is a myth that people lose their mental ability with age. What they have found is that people who don't continue to use their mental abilities—people who don't continue to learn and grow—lose their mental ability with age. Learning and growing is for everyone, young and old alike. Even during a boring task, you can find a way to engage your mind.

**During a dull task, move faster
or listen to something.**

"I Don't Know What to Do With My Life"

THERE *IS* SOMETHING you can do that would make you happy and make you a good living. You may not believe that, and in fact, it's not true. But it's not false either. It is only a useful idea to hold as you try to find your mission in life. Holding that idea will help it come true.

The perfect career for you: 1) needs to be something you like to do, and 2) it will have to be something worthwhile—something needed and wanted in the world.

If you don't like to do your work, you won't be happy, even when you're off work. Not only that, but you aren't likely to work hard enough at it to succeed. And if your work isn't worthwhile, it'll feel as though life is empty and has no meaning.

Here is a powerful method of discovering what your mission is: For the next two weeks, every time you notice you're feeling good about life and about yourself, take a moment to write out the answers to the following questions:

1. Where are you?
2. What are you doing?
3. Who are you with?

GET AS MANY of these written "snapshots" as you can in the next two or three weeks. Then go through them and see if you can find the commonalities. What are some general themes common to most or all of them? Try to find out what actions make you happy. Happiness is an indicator of where your interests and purposes lie buried. It sometimes helps to have a trusted friend look them over too. She might see something you don't see.

Remember Ernest Shackleton, the expedition leader of the ship *Endurance*? When he was young, a shipmate of his wrote:

> When he was on the subject that...appealed to his imagination, his voice changed to a deep vibrant tone, his features worked, his eyes shone, and his whole body seemed to have received an increase of vitality...Shackleton on these occasions...was not even the same man who

perhaps ten minutes earlier was spouting lines
from Keats or Browning...

THIS IS AN excellent description of what someone can
see from the outside. When you're talking about a
subject related to your strongest interest, people can see
it—you come alive! Ask your friends to not only look at
your notebook, but to *tell you* when they notice you
brighten up significantly. It will give you a good indication of where your strongest interests lie.

Whatever you find as a theme common to the times
you are happy and animated, you can assume it is in the
direction of your mission in life. It is in a direction that is
right for you.

Now *put more of it in your life.* Gradually add more
of it...maybe an hour of it every week for the next month
or two. Then make it two hours a week. Keep adding
more, pursuing your interest. The whole tone of your life
will rise, and you'll be happier.

**Find something you like to do that is needed
and wanted. Put more of it in your life.**

---

*Every job has some components which are
unrewarding, unfulfilling, and often tedious.
But there is no utopian job, no job made up
only of the things we love to do.*

— *Leo-Arthur Kelmenson*

Sometimes You Shouldn't Listen

WHEN WINSTON CHURCHILL was a young man, his father concluded that Winston was "unfit for a career in law or politics" because he did so badly in school.

Barbra Streisand's mother told her she wasn't pretty enough to be an actress and she could never become a singer because her voice wasn't good enough.

Conrad Hilton, who created a business empire with his Hilton Hotels, once overheard his father say to his mother: "Mary, I do *not* know what will become of Connie. I'm afraid he'll never amount to anything."

When Charles Darwin was getting ready to set sail on his five-year expedition on the *Beagle*, his father was extremely disappointed. He thought his son was drifting into a life of sin and idleness.

George Washington's mother was a harping, complaining, self-centered woman by all accounts. She belittled Washington's accomplishments and didn't show up at either of his presidential inaugurations. She was always whining that her children neglected her, and she was especially enraged when her son George ran off to command the army for the American Revolution. She honestly believed it was his duty to stay home and take care of her.

In his youth, the late Leonard Bernstein, one of the most talented and successful composers in American history, was continually pressured by his father to give up his music and do something worthwhile, like help out in his family's beauty-supply business. After Leonard became famous, his father was asked about that, and he answered, "Well how was I supposed to know he was *the* Leonard Bernstein?!"

People may criticize you or make fun of your ideas or actively try to stop you. Often their efforts are only attempts to protect you from failure. But failure is only a possibility *if you stop*. If you keep going, a "failure" is just another learning experience. And besides, giving up on a heartfelt aspiration is worse than failing. "Many people die," said Oliver Wendell Holmes, "with their music still in them." That's true tragedy.

So listen politely to the worries and criticisms of your friends and family, and do your best to put their minds at ease, but then carry on. Listen last to your own heart. You know yourself better than anyone on earth. Make sure your song is sung.

Listen to your own heart.
Don't let your music die with you.

Often they have struggled to gain
what society values instead of
developing their own personal values.
Gradually, life begins to seem empty,
the future hollow.

— Robert S. Eliot

Regret for the things we did can be tempered
by time; it is regret for the things we did not
do that is inconsolable.

— Sydney J. Harris

When an objective is meaningful, joy is a
natural consequence of its pursuit.

— Allen Wiesen

Just Keep Planting

PAUL ROKICH IS MY HERO. When Paul was a boy growing up in Utah, he happened to live near an old copper smelter, and the sulfur dioxide that poured out of the refinery had made a desolate wasteland out of what used to be a beautiful forest.

When a young visitor one day looked at this wasteland and saw that there was nothing living there—no animals, no trees, no grass, no bushes, no birds...nothing but fourteen thousand acres of black and barren land that even smelled bad—well, this kid looked at the land and said, "This place is crummy." Paul knocked him down. He felt insulted. But he looked around him and something happened inside him. He made a decision: Paul

Rokich vowed that some day he would bring back the life to this land.

Many years later Paul was in the area, and he went to the smelter office. He asked if they had any plans to bring the trees back. The answer was "No." He asked if they would let *him* try to bring the trees back. Again, the answer was "No." They didn't want him on their land. He realized he needed to be more knowledgeable before anyone would listen to him, so he went to college to study botany.

At the college he met a professor who was an expert in Utah's ecology. Unfortunately, this expert told Paul that the wasteland he wanted to bring back was beyond hope. He was told that his goal was foolish because even if he planted trees, and even if they grew, the wind would only blow the seeds forty feet per year, and that's all you'd get because there weren't any birds or squirrels to spread the seeds, and the seeds from *those* trees would need another thirty years before they started producing seeds of their own. Therefore, it would take approximately *twenty thousand years* to revegetate that six-square-mile piece of earth. His teachers told him it would be a waste of his life to try to do it. It just couldn't be done.

So he tried to go on with his life. He got a job operating heavy equipment, got married, and had some kids. But his dream would not die. He kept studying up on the subject, and he kept thinking about it. And then one night he got up and took some action. He did what he could with what he had. This was an important turning point. As Samuel Johnson wrote, "It is common to overlook what is near by keeping the eye fixed on something remote. In the same manner, present opportunities are neglected and attainable good is slighted by minds busied in extensive ranges." Paul stopped busying his mind in extensive ranges and looked at what opportunities for attainable good were right in front of him. Under the cover of darkness, he sneaked out into the wasteland with a backpack full of seedlings and started planting. For seven hours he planted seedlings.

He did it again a week later.

And every week, he made his secret journey into the wasteland and planted trees and shrubs and grass.

But most of it died.

For *fifteen years* he did this. When a whole valley of his fir seedlings burned to the ground because of a careless sheep-herder, Paul broke down and wept. Then he got up and kept planting.

Freezing winds and blistering heat, landslides and floods and fires destroyed his work time and time again. But he kept planting.

One night he found a highway crew had come and taken *tons* of dirt for a road grade, and all the plants he had painstakingly planted in that area were gone.

But he just kept planting.

Week after week, year after year he kept at it, against the opinion of the authorities, against the trespassing laws, against the devastation of road crews, against the wind and rain and heat...even against plain common sense. He just kept planting.

Slowly, *very* slowly, things began to take root. Then gophers appeared. Then rabbits. Then porcupines.

The old copper smelter eventually gave him permission, and later, as times were changing and there was political pressure to clean up the environment, the company actually *hired* Paul to do what he was already doing, and they provided him with machinery and crews to work with. Progress accelerated.

Now the place is fourteen thousand acres of trees and grass and bushes, rich with elk and eagles, and Paul Rokich has received almost every environmental award Utah has.

He says, "I thought that if I got this started, when I was dead and gone people would come and see it. I never thought *I'd* live to see it myself!"

It took him until his hair turned white, but he managed to keep that impossible vow he made to himself as a child.

What was it *you* wanted to do that you thought was impossible? Paul's story sure gives a perspective on things, doesn't it?

The way you get something accomplished in this world is to just keep planting. Just keep working. Just keep plugging away at it one day at a time for a long time, no matter who criticizes you, no matter how long it takes, no matter how many times you fall.

Get back up again. And just keep planting.

Just keep planting.

Getting Paid to Meditate

IN MOST DISCIPLINES of meditation, the first thing a student learns is how to concentrate. The Master gives the students techniques. In some cases, students may be instructed to count their breath. In other cases, they are given a word to repeat over and over. Sometimes they hold a visual image in the mind's eye or focus all their thoughts on a candle's flame.

There are hundreds of different techniques, but they all have one aim in mind: to teach students to hold their attention on one thing and prevent their attention from wandering away to other, more interesting things.

But this is America. The meditation practice of sitting still for long periods of time may have been perfectly appropriate for an unmarried, childless Brahmin priest who was a member of a caste that was supported by the government, but you and I have to make our own living. We don't have such an enormous privilege of time and guaranteed income. We need to be up and doing. And there's a lot to be done.

The ability to concentrate is the core ability, the essential skill. Control your attention and you control your mind. But the discipline to control your attention doesn't have to be done sitting still. It can be done with anything—*including your job.*

Your job can become a "spiritual" discipline. The practice is simply to keep your attention on your work. And unless it's a challenging part of your job that compels your attention, your mind will tend to wander, just as it does in meditation. You'll get distracted. You may get sidetracked with a daydream or playing a computer game or talking on the phone. In some studies, researchers found that while people were at work, fully 25 percent of the time *they weren't actually working.*

The practice of meditation is to bring the mind back to the task every time it wanders. Over and over and over again. This is meditation.

Do that with your work, and you are meditating. Do it often and you will slowly but steadily increase your ability to concentrate.

You can make any job challenging with this technique. Let's call it the Productive Meditation Technique. Simply do your job with the intention of paying attention to what you're supposed to be doing. When you notice you have gotten off track, get back to the purpose. Get crystal clear on the purpose and function of your job and the part it plays in the overall scheme of things, and then pay that purpose all of your attention. Your mind *will* wander. When you notice you've strayed from the purpose, bring yourself back. Again and again.

Then take the practice home. Sweep the floors or listen to someone you love *as a meditation.* Whenever your thoughts wander, bring them back. Practice mowing the lawn with your full attention. Cook dinner with your full attention. Talk to your child with your full attention.

This ability to keep your mind here in this moment is not a trivial skill. It may not get you reincarnated as a higher being, but it will make you more alive right here and now.

**When you notice your mind has wandered,
bring it back to the task at hand.**

---

*No one can do more for you than your
own purified mind—no parent, no relative,
no friend, no one. A well-disciplined
mind brings happiness.*

— Buddha

Be More Energetic

ENERGY IS A BEAUTIFUL THING. A person with a lot of energy can accomplish twice what someone without much energy can and have more fun doing it. You get more *life* with more energy. And here's a way to crank up your engine: Act more energetic. That sounds like shallow, positive-thinking hype, but it's actually based on solid evidence: It works.

When you act more energetic, it stimulates your body. Lying down is relaxing. Moving around is more stimulating. Moving around quickly is even more stimulating. It gets the heart pumping. It puts the mind in gear.

Our biology has evolved to fit a different kind of world than the one in which we now find ourselves. There were plenty of times in our prehistory when food was scarce. People who wantonly used up energy would be the first to die, leaving no offspring. The bodies following the prime directive CONSERVE ENERGY passed their genes to us.

But times have changed. It's no longer difficult to find food. If anything, food is difficult to avoid. Calories are everywhere, hugely and abundantly available. As a matter of fact, now a major concern for people in America is being overweight. Times have changed dramatically. There's no longer any need to conserve energy, but your genes don't know it. They've still got their orders, like a soldier in a jungle who was never told the war is over.

You *can* be more energetic, but you'll have to override your feelings. And you can do this. You'll have to essentially ignore the natural laziness we all share.

The way to override your body's prime directive is to *act* energetic whether you feel like it or not.

The truth is, you *are* energetic when you act that way, regardless of how you feel. Listen to what I'm saying here. You want to be more energetic? By simply acting more energetic, you immediately become more energetic *in reality,* in the same way that when you *act* ethical, you *are* ethical, regardless of whether or not you were tempted to do the wrong thing.

You can become more energetic in ten seconds. Simply start acting more energetic.

You don't have to *feel* energetic to *be* energetic. A nice bonus, however, is that often when you act energetic, it will rev you up and make you *feel* energetic too.

Experiments show that when people walk quickly, it speeds up their metabolism, making them feel more energetic, and this energetic feeling lasts for several hours after the activity. Acting energetic physically changes your body into a more energetic body.

So don't wait until you feel energetic before you act. Act first. The feelings will follow.

Act more energetic.

---

*[After pushing past fatigue, we] find
amounts of ease and power that we never
dreamed ourselves to own, sources of strength
habitually not taxed, because habitually we
never push through the obstruction of fatigue.*

— *William James*

*Things may come to those who wait, but only
the things left by those who hustle.*

— *Abraham Lincoln*

Burn Your Own BTUs

MIHALY CSIKSZENTMIHALYI has been doing some fascinating research into creativity and enjoyment at the University of Chicago for over thirty years now. He invented a new way to study enjoyment. It's called the Experience Sampling Method.

Basically, subjects are given a pager and a booklet, and then they go about their normal lives. At random intervals eight times each day, the pager goes off. The subjects immediately stop what they're doing and fill out the questionnaire in the booklet.

Each questionnaire is identical. It asks what they're doing, where they are, and who they're with. Then it asks them to mark where they are on several scales of experience, such as one to seven to indicate where they are from "happy" to "very sad."

After collecting over a hundred thousand of these samples, Csikszentmihalyi had a huge fund of raw information. He began to wonder, "Are people happier when they use more material resources in their leisure activities? Or are they happier when they invest more of themselves?" In other words his question was, "If I spend my day off going to a movie and out to dinner (or using resources and electricity in some way), will I have a more enjoyable day off than I would if I spent the day gardening or reading or talking or doing something requiring just my own effort?"

Which is ultimately more enjoyable? Using energy outside yourself, or using your own energy?

What would you guess? To answer the question, Csikszentmihalyi and his colleagues went back through the data and sorted each experience sample by the amount of energy being used. They measured the material resources in units of energy called BTUs (British Thermal Units, the energy it takes to raise one pound of water one degree Fahrenheit) and sifted the data in search of an answer.

What they found surprised everyone. The *fewer* BTUs a person used in his leisure, the *more* he enjoyed it. Those time-off activities like watching TV, driving, boating, or anything that used electricity or expensive equipment were *less* enjoyable than self-powered activities like conversing with a friend, working on a hobby, training a dog, or gardening. This goes against the prevailing notions of what's enjoyable. "Everybody knows" it would be more fun cruising on a yacht drinking margaritas than building a bookshelf in your basement. "Everybody knows" it would be more fun to go to the movies than it would to sit home and read a book. But according to the research, that's not the case. Certainly those high-BTU activities are easier and more immediately appealing. But not more enjoyable.

When the pager went off and the participants stopped and checked how much they were enjoying what they were doing, they discovered something truly illuminating: The *most* fun things *don't cost much.*

Is this true for you? Test it. On your next two days off, do something that uses up material resources the first day, and the next day, have a friend over and converse or do something powered by your own energy. You'll see a difference. The activity might not be as titillating at the moment, but when your day is done, you'll be more satisfied with the self-powered day.

Do you want some first-class leisure? Find an interest and pursue it. Turn off the TV and use your own energy. You may be surprised to find it doesn't wear you out but fully refreshes you.

This is extremely good news. It's good for your pocketbook, it's good for the planet, *and* it's good for your own enjoyment. Use more of *your own* BTUs on your time off and the world will be a better place.

Use your own energy during your leisure time.

How to Earn More Money

WHETHER YOU OWN your own company or work for someone else, you can earn more than you now earn. The first question to ask yourself is "Am I providing a product or service that is both wanted and needed?" When the answer is yes, you can earn more money by *increasing either the quality or the quantity of your service.*

The hardest part of increasing your service is *thinking up* ways to do it. Sure, if you work faster and put in more hours, you will increase your service. And if you take more care and pay more attention to your work, you will certainly increase the quality. Those are obvious. But there will come a time when these things cannot be increased any more: There are only twenty-four hours in a day, there are physical limits to how fast you can move, and you can give no more attention to your work once you are giving it all your attention.

But it is possible to think of other ways to increase your service. It will only take some thinking. Sit down ten different times in the next month and each time think up three different ways you could increase your service. Allow your imagination to go wild. At the end of the month, pick the best one and *do it*.

Another thing you can do to increase your earnings is to read books and listen to tapes related to your line of work, your health, or your ability to deal with people. Learn more about these three topics and it will help you earn more.

The first subject to study is the specific area or industry you work in. Every field has a history. How did it start? Who were the principle originators? And that's just the beginning. The libraries and bookstores are full of books and tapes and videotapes on every conceivable subject. Study not only background, but also information that will make you better at your job. Take night classes. Listen to tapes in your car. Educate yourself. As you learn, you become more of an expert. Generally speaking, the more of an expert you are in your field, the more useful you are. And the more useful you are, the more money you can make.

Learning ways to increase your level of health will help you in two ways: First, your level of energy is closely tied to your level of health, and you can do more work with a high energy level. Second, when you have better health, you tend to have better relationships with people. Have you ever noticed how difficult it is to be nice to people when you feel like hell? Our health affects our moods, and our moods affect our relationships with others. And people who get along well with others, according to the research, make more money than those who don't. Their relationships are better with their bosses and with their assistants. They get more cooperation and consideration. In the long run, this adds up to more money.

Which brings us to the third area to study: people. As far as I can tell, there is no final attainment in this area. I've been actively improving my ability to deal with people for about twenty-two years now (and I was pretty good when I started), and I'm nowhere near as good as I could be. In other words, I can profitably continue to improve my ability to deal with people for the rest of my life, and I'll bet the same is true for you.

Learn about your line of work, read up on how to maintain good health, and constantly practice the fine art of dealing with people. These are lifetime studies. And do the hard work of thinking up ways to increase the quantity and quality of the service you provide. Do these things and you will earn more money.

To earn more money:
Increase your service, and continue to learn about your work, good health, and people.

The Trouble With Troublemakers

WHEN SOMEONE AT WORK talks badly about you behind your back, puts you down, interferes with your work, makes you mad, or otherwise makes trouble for you, the natural tendency is to focus on *them*. You want to get back at them. You want to talk badly about them behind *their* back, put *them* down, make trouble for *them* in some way.

But I want you to consider the possibility that returning like for like is a mistake. Look at the three practical steps below—all of them effective ways to deal with troublemakers—and notice: None involve talking about, thinking about, or speaking with the troublemakers themselves, because that doesn't work. Here's what *does* work:

1. **Do your work extremely well**. Think of your level of excellence as a sliding scale, from doing-as-little-as-you-can-do-without-getting-fired all the way up to doing-your-very-best-every-second-you-are-at-work. At any given moment, you are somewhere between those two extremes. Move yourself further up the scale and you will feel more confident of your position. Doing your work well counteracts the feelings of insecurity a troublemaker can cause.

2. **Keep your integrity level high**. Doing anything unethical will increase the insecurity you feel. Conversely, the more you act with honesty and fairness, the better you will feel about yourself and about your position at work.

3. **Stay in good communication with everyone else**. A common response to feeling that someone is out to get you is to withdraw. But that's a big mistake. The universe of human opinion abhors a vacuum, and if a troublemaker says something bad about you and the listener hears nothing from you, guess what? The slanderous information will tend to hold the floor from lack of any other viewpoint. Your bosses and coworkers may be mature, rational people, but human emotions still influence their decisions, opinions, and conclusions. Stay in communication with people—not trying to prove anything, but just

being yourself—and the reality of who you are will help negate any rumors about you.

DO THESE THREE and the threat from the troublemaker will be minimized. You can't really get rid of such an element for good. That's the trouble with troublemakers. They are bound to crop up now and then, as inevitably as a bad storm. If you try to argue with them or fight with them or use their tactics on them, you will lose. They've been at it longer than you.

Do your work to the best of your ability, conduct yourself honorably, and stay in good communication. Your position will be solid and the storm will pass over you without so much as a shudder.

To handle a troublemaker at work:
Do your work exceptionally well, keep your integrity level high, and stay in good communication with everyone else.

I have known a vast quantity of nonsense talked about bad men not looking you in the face. Don't trust that conventional idea. Dishonesty will stare honesty out of countenance any day of the week, if there is anything to be got by it.

— Charles Dickens

The Spirit of the Games

I'VE ALWAYS HAD A DISTASTE for competition. I never liked the feeling of trying to outdo another person. But competition is a fact of life, from the lowliest worms to the executive on Wall Street. Competition is like gravity. We may not like it, but there it is anyway, having its effect on our lives, regardless of what we may think about it. There's nothing nasty about it—gravity doesn't care whether you hurt yourself when you fall or not.

If you have two organisms competing for a limited resource, say, a lion and a hyena competing for the carcass of a gazelle, if the lion doesn't want to compete or feels competition is wrong, then the hyena will eat and the lion will go hungry. If this goes on, the lion will die of starvation and the hyena will have many offspring. Nature is not being cruel. Competition is the way of the world. It's the way life on this planet became so complex and beautiful and amazing. It's the way your incredible brain evolved. Ultimately, competition is good. It makes things better. It forces improvement.

I'm a writer. There are places that pay for writing. And there are other writers in the world who would prefer that the money paid for that skill go into their bank account rather than mine. The money can't really go to every writer's bank account. There's a selection going on. Certain things will be selected for and certain things will be selected against. It *is* a competition, whether I want to acknowledge that fact or not. And, of course, the ones who compete the best will *always* out-compete the ones who don't compete as well.

Competition can be an ugly affair, typified by the presidential elections with all the mudslinging and back-stabbing. Although that's obviously competition, so is what goes on at the Olympics.

The presidential elections are ugly, but the Olympics are beautiful—whether you win or lose, you can still shake the hand of your competitor in friendship. You can compete with honor. You can compete for noble reasons. You can compete for the sake of others or for a cause you believe in. The Spirit of the Games raises competition to the elevated place it should hold.

Consider it in this light and you can learn to appreciate competition. It's important because you must either compete well, or those dreams you have will not happen. Whatever your job, this is true. If you've had, like me, a distaste for competition, start changing your attitude. Learn to appreciate and even like competition. Because the truth is, if you can compete well, you can fulfill your desires. If you can't or don't compete well, or if you don't "play the game" at all, someone else will get the raise or promotion or position, someone else's view will hold the floor, someone else's vision will be realized, and your dreams will become pipe dreams. It's up to you. You can compete, play well, and know you've done your best, or not. It's your call.

Learn to like competition
and compete with honor.

You cannot believe in honor until you have achieved it. Better keep yourself clean and bright: you are the window through which you must see the world.

— *George Bernard Shaw*

It is useless for sheep to pass resolutions in favor of vegetarianism while wolves remain of a different opinion.

— *William Ralph Inge*

A Lasting State of Feeling Great

THE ENGLISH POET AND CLERGYMAN Charles Kingsley wrote, "We act as though comfort and luxury were the chief requirements of life, when all we need to make us happy is something to be enthusiastic about." He was right. When you have something to be enthusiastic about, you can be in a good mood almost all the time.

If your job doesn't make you enthusiastic, you're probably stressed or tired when you come home and just want to watch a little TV and relax. But relaxing will never make you feel happy and fully alive. Naturally, you could make plans to do something this weekend, and you might be thoroughly enthusiastic about it all week. But then Monday comes and back in the grind you go.

What you really need is something *ongoing* to be enthusiastic about. What you need is a challenging and compelling *purpose*.

Up until a century ago, simple survival provided just such a purpose for most people, and that's still the case in much of the world. But for most of us in this country, it's no longer a challenge to merely survive. We have tamed our world. More than likely, the only way you will ever be challenged by a compelling purpose is if *you* create one deliberately. And if this purpose is going to make you truly *enthusiastic*, it needs to be something that *personally* compels you—some subject or task you think is fascinating or feel is vitally important.

Pursue your purpose with vigor and you will be in a good mood most of the time. Things that bother most people won't bother you as much. You'll still have your ups and downs, but they will occur in a higher range. You'll still have to deal with problems, but you will handle them better. And your improved attitude will make your relationships happier and more harmonious. When you have something ongoing in your life that you are enthusiastic about, *the quality of your life is better*.

Pursuing a purpose is not comfortable, restful or easy. But it's great fun! It makes life deeply enjoyable. Watching TV is enticing, sure. It calls. It beckons. But it won't fulfill you or make you happy. A purpose will.

Find a purpose you're enthusiastic about and get to it.

You Create Yourself

I WAS TRYING TO WORK yesterday, but I was tired. I had stayed up late and gotten up late and I felt "off." When I realized what was happening, I decided to get back on track. I started paying attention to my work. I looked people in the eye and spoke with purpose. I decided to be a person I respect—not some victim to my feelings or circumstances, but a creator of who I am. I set a standard for myself and then lived up to it in behavior. And my feelings came around. I stopped feeling so tired. I started feeling more purposeful. But even if my feelings didn't come around, and they sometimes don't, it wouldn't matter. I can look people in the eye even when I don't feel like it.

You can do this too. It's not like I have any great amount of self-discipline or willpower. You can set standards for yourself and then live up to those standards, even when you don't feel like it.

Let's not be the effect of our feelings. They change too much. Set *physical standards* for yourself: What you will DO, not what you will feel. *Act* ethically. *Speak* with intention. *Exercise* even when you don't feel like it. You cannot choose how you will feel voluntarily, but you can always choose what you will *do*.

Then, regardless of your upbringing or past habits or how much you drank the night before or the argument you had with your spouse this morning, *take the actions you want to take*. Be who you choose to be. It's up to you. You are what you decide you are at any given moment—not how you feel, not how you were raised. Those are defaults, like the defaults on a word processor, and can be overridden at any time by a conscious decision. On some days, your defaults may be perfectly good because the circumstances and your feelings line up to make you act exactly as you wish. But the rest of the time, *you'll* have to take over the controls.

Decide how you want to act, and act that way. You create yourself.

Decide how you want to act and act that way.

Wasting Time... The Old-Fashioned Way

RESEARCHERS PUT SOME RATS in plain cages, each one alone. Then they put some rats in bigger cages with other rats and toys to play with. The ones in the "enriched environment" grew smarter (they learned mazes faster). And when the researchers cut open their brains, they found that the rats in the enriched environment had bigger and heavier brains because they had more dendrites (connections between brain cells).

Mental ability—for rats as well as people—doesn't depend on the number of brain cells, but on the number of connections between those brain cells. And the stimulation of play increases the number of connections.

To refine their understanding, researchers then put some rats in an enriched environment and some other rats in a position so they could *watch* the rats in the enriched environment. What they found is revealing: The ones who watched didn't get any smarter and their brains grew no bigger.

Preliminary studies on people are finding the same thing: Something about playing games increases brain power. But *watching* people play games doesn't do it.

And playing games usually gets you face to face with people, talking to them. We are social creatures, and we are healthier and happier when we have enough enjoyable social contact. Passive entertainment like television doesn't encourage much interaction. The television programmers and the people who design the commercials don't want you to turn away from your TV and talk to your spouse. You might miss a commercial. So they try to keep it as lively and appealing as possible. The end result is people can "be together" for hours on end without talking to each other. This doesn't satisfy our need for sociability.

So...playing games can increase the connections between brains cells and between people.

But we all know games are a waste of time. The problem is, we *do* waste our time. We watch TV and movies. We waste hours. Apparently we have a *need* to waste time, or at least to spend time doing something other than working, even when our work is enjoyable.

Since passive entertainment like watching TV doesn't seem to enrich our minds and playing games does, here's the bottom line: *Games are a better waste of time than TV or movies*.

Here are two tips for replacing some of your TV time with games:

1. **Mix it up**. Different games require different skills. Your partners will be good at some, lousy at others. Mix it up and you won't win or lose all the time and you'll get better in areas in which you are now weak.

2. **Play games you think are fun**. The games that are likely to do you the most good are the ones you think are fun. If chess isn't fun for you, regardless of its stature in the gleaming world of the sophisticated set, don't start there. Be guided by one criterion: Fun.

YOU DON'T NEED to find games that stretch your mind. You don't need to *make* a game "do you some good." As long as you're having fun, it *is* doing you some good. *The benefit is in the fun*. If you're concentrating too hard on trying to do something good for yourself, it won't be as much fun, so it won't be as good for you.

So relax and enjoy yourself. Replace some of your TV time with game playing, and you'll be better off.

**Replace some of your TV time
with game playing.**

Taking Credit

WHEN YOU DON'T TAKE CREDIT for things you do right or well, it can cause a mild but debilitating form of depression. You might not mope around, but you won't feel as enthusiastic toward life as you could.

When you don't acknowledge yourself for what you've accomplished, you get the *feeling* that you haven't really done anything, and since you know you spent the day doing stuff, your efforts seem pointless and futile.

The solution is to make it a practice to ask yourself this question: *What can I take credit for?* Think of anything in your life that you're *glad* happened, and look to see how much of it you can take credit for. What part of it was because of what *you* did? Until you're in the habit, force yourself to do this every day. Ask yourself that question several times a day, and try to start noticing this simple fact: Much of the good stuff that happens in your life is a result of *your* choices and *your* effort.

If you're not already in the habit of doing this, here's what will happen: Over time, your level of energy and feeling of power and effectiveness will experience a resurgence. Your estimation of your own self-worth will rise up to match your actual worth. You will become more enthusiastic toward life. You'll have the feeling that you have been spinning your wheels for a long time and suddenly the wheels are gripping the solid ground firmly and you are *moving*.

Take credit where credit is due. It may be impolite to brag to other people, but it is sane and healthy to acknowledge your own accomplishments to yourself.

Ask yourself, "What can I take credit for?"

People who believe they cause good things tend to like themselves better than people who believe good things come from other people or circumstances.

— Martin Seligman

Make It Happen

IN THE REMOTE JUNGLES of Southeast Asia on the Malay Peninsula, aboriginal tribes were studied in the 1930s and '40s. Two of the tribes—the Negritos and the Temiar—were very similar. They both paid a lot of attention to their dreams.

The Negritos' attitude was passive. They felt they were the victims of evil forces. If they had a bad dream about a tree, for example, from that point on they would be afraid of the tree and its evil spirit.

But the Temiar taught their children that aggression in dreams was good. The child should not turn away from dream monsters, but attack them. They were taught that if they run away, the monsters or evil spirits will plague them until they turn and fight.

The two tribes were similar in many ways, but this one difference made the Temiar psychologically healthy, according to Kilton Stewart and Pat Noone, a psychologist and an anthropologist who studied them, and it made the Negritos psychologically *un*healthy.

In any situation, you can have the attitude of reaching, of trying to accomplish what you want, or by default you will become a victim, the effect of circumstances and other people's goals. If you aren't actively trying to cause an effect you want, you will be forced by the aggression of others to respond, to react, to be the effect of their initiations. It isn't the perfect design by my standards, but that is the way it works out, whether we like it or not.

So make it a practice to think about what you want, what you think would be good, and then try to make that happen. You'll run into resistance sometimes. That's okay. No need to resist the resistance. It's just someone else trying to make something happen too (or trying to prevent themselves from being a victim). Don't get caught up in it. Keep in mind what you want and continue taking steps toward it.

In other words, become less passive and more aggressive in your attitude.

Aggression can be a good thing. If it's aggression without anger or judgement, it can create a lot of good in the world. In fact, it has already.

**Think about what you want
and try to make it happen.**

Forbidden Fruits

HAVE YOU EVER HAD THE EXPERIENCE, during a power outage or on a vacation, of finally having the time to really enjoy a conversation or read a good book and find yourself thinking, "Why don't I do that more often?"

Why? Because the easy entertainments and products of our modern world are always enticing, and, of course, there are always chores that need to be done.

Some famous authors have written their books while in jail. I've often thought what a great opportunity they had. They lived in circumstances highly conducive to writing (because there wasn't much else to do). And here I am, stuck in civilization with all its temptations. Poor little me.

But there *is* a way to create some of the same kinds of experiences without power outages or jail time. Human beings have been successfully using a simple and very effective method for thousands of years. It is simply to *forbid* things.

Today, for example, I have forbidden TV for myself. And I've already written more today than I have in the last week. It works. And there's nothing forced about it. I don't feel I *have* to write. I want to. Once I take away the nonstop seduction of the television, the most interesting and fun thing available is writing. Forbidding a distraction simply opens up the time I have available to do the things I really want.

Try it. Take the thing you do that wastes the most time or creates the lowest-quality experience and forbid it for a day. You don't have to make it permanent. Simply forbid it for tomorrow or for the rest of today. I think you'll like the result.

Forbid something for the day.

---

*Lost time is never found again, and what
we call time enough always proves little
enough. Let us then be up and doing,
and doing to a purpose.*

— Benjamin Franklin

Life is a Meditation...

...AND MEDITATION IS A METAPHOR for life. Meditation consists of keeping your mind on one thing. Of course, what happens is your mind drifts onto other things. You notice your mind has drifted, you're tempted to keep thinking about it, but then you let it go and bring yourself back to your meditation.

Although life is a little more complicated, it is much the same: You notice you've gone off the track and you get back on.

You can't have it all, do it all or be it all. To live happily, you have to narrow your purposes down to a few: certain relationships, certain important values, and a general purpose for your life. Then the world and your own mind/body will continually take you off onto side-trips and distractions. Salespeople, in-laws, your desire for diversions and pleasures and entertainments, advertisers, people who want something from you (like your attention), and many more sources of distraction are constantly coming your way.

So you get off purpose. And then you notice you've gone off on a purpose that has nothing to do with what's important to you, and you let it go and get back to your own purposes.

For example, I was doing some work in my living room one hot summer night and I wasn't wearing a shirt. Two teenage boys skateboarding by across the street looked in my window and one of them said, "Hey, put on a shirt!" I was being invaded in my own living room. He said it again. It was clearly wrong, and I wanted to go over there and wring their scrawny little necks, or at least call the police, or do *something* that would show those two punks they can't get away with that with *me*! But all of that has nothing to do with my chosen purposes. No real harm was done. It was simply another opportunity to either get off track or let it go and get back to my work.

Make your entire life a meditation. Less of your time will be wasted on things that aren't important to you and more of *your* goals will be achieved.

Notice when you're drifting away from your *own* purposes, and then get back on track.

Vocabulary Raises

AS ONE CLASS GRADUATED from a large university, a group of researchers gave them an English vocabulary test and then tracked those people for twenty years. Strange as it may seem, those who knew the definitions of the most words were in the highest income group twenty years later. The researchers discovered that the people who, in the beginning, had the worst vocabulary scores were in the lowest income group twenty years later. There wasn't a single exception. Does that or doesn't that strike you as utterly astounding?

Could this really be true? And can we extrapolate the conclusion that if you started now and increased your vocabulary, your efforts could eventually put you in a higher income group than you would have been in otherwise? Let's look further.

In another study, the executive and supervisory personnel of thirty-nine manufacturing plants were given extensive testing. All of them, from the lowest level of supervisor to the top of the executive elite rated higher than average on leadership qualities. Between all the leaders, there was a close similarity in leadership ability. But there were striking differences on the *vocabulary* test. Basically, the higher the person's score on the vocabulary test, the higher their position in that company. The presidents and vice presidents of the companies had an average score of 236 (a perfect score was 272). The average score for superintendents was 140. Foremen averaged 114.

Why? What's going on here?

Let's look at it this way: When you were young, you didn't know the definitions of very many words, so you didn't understand much of what people around you were saying. As you learned more words, your understanding grew. Knowing the definition of even one more word makes a difference because if there is only one word you don't know, you'll often miss more of what's being said than that one word. The word is part of a sentence that you won't completely understand. The sentence is part of a paragraph. One unknown word can create a small gap in your understanding of the entire subject.

The most obvious way to prevent that gap is to always look up a word you don't know. The bad news is that you can't really do that while listening to a lecture and most people don't like interrupting themselves when they're reading to stop and look up a word. I know I don't. So the word doesn't get looked up, and some of the ideas are only partially understood because of it. The larger your vocabulary, the less that happens and the more you understand what you read and hear.

The good news is that after you know a word, you are more likely to understand any sentence with that word in it *for the rest of your life*. Any effort you make to increase the number of definitions you know will have a far-reaching and long-lasting effect. Here are three ways you can improve your vocabulary:

1. When you read a word you aren't sure of, look it up. Then create two or three sentences with that word in it. Using the word in your own self-created sentence is the quickest way to cement that word in your memory.

2. Get vocabulary tapes for your car and listen to them while driving, speaking the words out loud (it makes it easier to remember how to pronounce them).

3. Buy or make vocabulary flash cards and keep some in your pocket to test yourself in spare moments—while waiting in line, for example. You can pick one every morning and carry the

card with you to work, trying to use that word in several sentences that day.

TAKE THESE THREE steps and, in an adscititious manner, you may just see your income go from a flat line to an upwardly pointing falciform in the vespertine years of your life. Sticks and stones may break your bones, but words may get you a promotion.

adscititious: added, supplemental, additional
falciform: in the shape of a sickle, curved
vespertine: pertaining to the evening
    —Webster's New Universal Unabridged Dictionary

To increase your vocabulary:
Look up words, listen to vocabulary tapes, and use vocabulary flash cards.

It is impossible to fit in and stand out at the same time.

— Will Bowen

Play the Game

YOUR JOB IS NOT A GAME. But when you approach it like a game, you'll enjoy it more and you're more likely to be successful at it.

Research at the University of Chicago shows that games produce a condition called *flow*, characterized by absorption in the activity (a lack of thoughts about anything else), a feeling of control, and enjoyment. And one of the most common characteristics of flow is that time seems to fly.

According to the principle researcher, Mihaly Csikszentmihalyi, one of the reasons games produce flow is that the outcome of the game is *not* important. We may really get into a game and the outcome may seem very important at the time, but we know nothing is really at stake. We won't lose the mortgage, nobody will die, the college scholarship for our kids won't be jeopardized.

But at work, there *is* something at stake. That means when we're working, we tend to pay attention to where the work is *getting* us. What this means is that work becomes a means to an end and that means the end of flow because a *requirement* of the experience of flow is an involvement in the activity itself—a lack of thoughts about anything else. When a person is looking at the clock or thinking about her position or promotion in the company, it's enough of a distraction to prevent flow. Even wondering if you're enjoying yourself is a distraction. *Absorption* produces flow.

Of course, when most people are working, they are working for money. So the work is done as a means to an end. Does that mean we can't experience flow at work? Luckily, no. Even when you do something as a means to an end, you can learn to become absorbed in the work and forget about where it is getting you *while* you're doing it.

If you want to experience more flow on the job, then, simply learn to become more engrossed in your work. Learn to "get into it."

If your job is stressful or boring, however, becoming absorbed is difficult. If what you've got is stress, that means the challenge of your job, either physically or psychologically, is greater than your skills. The answer is to find out what skill you need to improve and work on that. *Increase your skill.* That's the answer to stress.

At the other end of the spectrum is boredom. If your job is boring, you'll have to find a way to make the work more challenging, interesting, or creative. It may take you a lot of thinking to figure out how to do that, but keep at it and you can find a way.

For example, during his research, Csikszentmihalyi found a man working on an assembly line, doing the same thing over and over every day, who had found a way to experience flow in a potentially boring job. He approached the task like an Olympic athlete, carefully working out ways to trim the time it took him to complete each task. By timing himself and shaving off seconds, he had become the most competent man on the line, but more important for our discussion here, he *enjoyed* his work more than anyone on the line. And he wasn't focusing on trying to get a raise or gaining the approval of his supervisor. He was engrossed in beating his personal best.

Find a way to become absorbed. You'll enjoy your work more. Get so engrossed in your work that you forget about everything else, like where it's getting you. It'll get you a lot further that way.

Get so engrossed in your work
that you forget about everything else.

Self-Help

WILLIAM MILLER, A RESEARCHER in the alcohol-treatment field, wanted to find out what kind of treatment would work best for controlling problem drinking. He divided his experimental subjects into two groups and tested the treatment group with a variety of methods, including Antabuse (a drug that makes you sick if you drink) and counseling.

That was the treatment group. But researchers always need a control group when they test the effectiveness of a therapy. They need a baseline of results to compare to the results of the experimental group. The control group was merely given a short self-help manual and told to read it and do their best.

Many of the treatments worked very well. But, Miller says, "To our amazement, people in the control group did just as well as the treatment group." They thought maybe they had flubbed the study somehow, so they repeated it and got the same results. Still skeptical, they repeated the experiment again and, once again, they got the same results.

People who simply took a short self-help book home were just as capable of moderating their drinking as those who received the expensive and more extensive treatment. Why?

Much of the most effective part of therapy is simply convincing clients to change and telling them how, which is of course something the therapist could put in a book. The changes you make in your life have to be made by *you*. Even good therapy is largely dependent on the client's self-help.

Practical written advice can be as effective as the most expensive help you can find because the two ways to improve your life are:

1) do something different
2) think something different

And written material can help you accomplish both of those. All you need is a little motivation, and a book can furnish you with that too.

This book you now have in your hands may look inert. It may seem commonplace and ordinary. But it can really help you change your life! Use the ideas. Improve

your actions and the way you think. Use it as a spur to
your own motivation. You can make your life better—no
kidding. Are you interested? Help yourself.

Make your life better by reading helpful books.

---

*The poorest man in the world is the
man limited to his own experience,
the man who does not read.*

— Daniel N. Fader

*If you don't read about things that interest you,
you won't have any interest in reading.*

— Adam Khan

*The person who doesn't read has no advantage
over the person who doesn't know how.*

— Proverb

Speedy Reading— One Chunk at a Time

THE ABILITY TO READ FAST is made up of lots of little skills. You can use as many or as few of those skills as you want. The more of those individual skills you use, the faster you'll be able to read. Add all the skills together, and sure, it's dramatic. But who needs dramatics? A small improvement is cool enough.

Of course, when you learn to read faster, you can read more. But there's another benefit that's not so obvious: Reading will become more *interesting*. You find the same difference between hearing a lecturer who speaks too slowly versus one who speaks at a comfortable but lively pace. It's more interesting. It's more fun. It keeps you awake. And by reading faster, you're making the process more challenging in a controlled way. And a challenge that is *under your control* is enjoyable.

Below are three basic techniques for increasing your speed. Pick one and try it in the spirit of fun. When you've got that one going pretty well, come back and add another one. After awhile, you'll have increased your speed...and probably your comprehension too (studies show speed alone can increase your comprehension).

Here are the techniques:

1. **Don't let your eyes regress.** Keep them moving forward. They will have a tendency to go back a few words occasionally. That continual little movement backwards adds up. If you stop doing it, your speed will increase a little. Studies indicate that rereading words like that doesn't increase comprehension anyway.

2. **Constantly practice "picking up speed"** as you read. Reading is a skill, and like any other skill, the constant effort to do it a little better keeps you getting better and better at it as time goes on.

3. **Take in more words at a time.** If you normally see two words at a time when you read, your eyes look at two words, move to the next two and stop to look at those, move to the next two, etc. Begin taking in three words at a time

so your eyes make fewer stops, increasing your speed. Increase your challenge only as your skill increases. Keep it fun. Don't push yourself so hard it becomes stressful.

WHEN YOU FIRST practice a technique, you'll be conscious of using it and that may very well distract you a little from comprehending what you're reading. But keep practicing and the technique will become automatic, no longer requiring your conscious attention, allowing you to put your full attention on the *content* of the written material. At that point, you will have gained an increase in reading skill to enjoy for the rest of your life.

To read faster and increase your comprehension:
Don't let your eyes regress,
practice picking up speed,
and take in more words at a time.

Properly we should read for power.
Man reading should be man intensely alive.
The book should be a ball of
light in one's hand.

— *Ezra Pound*

Thousand-Watt Bulb

HERE'S AN ODD SUGGESTION: When you're working, try to burn calories. Be useful, helpful, and as productive as you can. Even if your job is sitting at a keyboard all day, try to do it *energetically* and with enthusiasm. It may seem stupid, but give it a try before you decide. Blast out your effort like a thousand-watt bulb and here's what you'll get in return:

1. **You'll be *more* energetic, not less.** You'd think it would wear you out, but that's not the case, as you can find out for yourself by trying it. You may have a pleasant sense of relaxation

at the end of the day, as you would from some good exercise, but it won't make you tired. *Holding back* makes you tired. Going through the motions makes you tired. Just trying to get through the day makes you tired.

2. **You'll advance faster**. Of course, when opportunities come around, the person putting their all into the work (you, for instance) is going to be chosen over the people who are getting by doing as little as possible. Obviously.

3. **Your job will be more secure**. Giving your all will make you feel more secure in a sometimes insecure world. And you'll not only *feel* more secure, your feeling will be an accurate perception of the reality.

4. **You'll feel better about yourself**. It feels good to do well. And you can look your boss in the eye and know s/he's getting a good deal. You can see that there are very few people you work with (or none at all) who give their all. The comparison between you and the rest of the pack will make it very clear in your mind you can stand tall and proud when your supervisor is around.

5. **You'll improve your abilities faster**. Whatever skills your job requires will be honed more quickly when you're giving it your all.

THE HUMAN BRAIN and body has a default setting: Conserve energy. You know this from personal experience. It's probably hardwired genetically and kicks in with the onset of adulthood. You and I have a natural tendency to try to be conservative with our energy output. That's there naturally, but you're not stuck with it. You can override that default setting with a simple decision: Put out as much effort as you can.

Put the decision into action and before long, you'll forget. You'll be back to your default setting. When you notice you've gone back to the *conserve energy* mode, decide again to try to burn calories. Remake your decision again and again. Blasting out the energy won't wear you out or make you tired. But it *will* make you feel proud, secure, and confident.

When you're working, try to burn calories.

Unless a person is worth more than he's now receiving, he cannot move ahead— he's receiving all he's worth!

— *Earl Nightingale*

An Island of Order in a Sea of Chaos

THE MANAGER OF A LARGE RESTAURANT hired my wife and business partner, J. Klassy Evans, as a consultant. The manager was having problems that caused her a great deal of stress and she didn't know what to do about it. For example, no matter how many times the manager talked to certain employees, they continually showed up late for work and always had a good excuse.

Klassy suggested something simple: Every time a person shows up late, assign them a cleaning task to be completed before they go home that day.

It worked. Not only were fewer people showing up late, but a lot of things the manager wanted clean were getting clean. The restaurant was under better control and the manager was less distressed.

My son used to leave his window open and his heater on when he left for school in the morning. No matter how many times I told him to turn off his heater, he never seemed to remember. Saving my money wasn't very important to him. It's the vexing kind of problem commonly experienced by most parents. I decided to make it important to him and fined him one dollar from his allowance every time I found the heater on and the window open. Would you believe it? His memory made an immediate, complete, and permanent improvement after losing only one dollar!

You control yourself for the same reason you try to help your child develop self-control, and for the same reason a manager tries to maintain order with her staff: A person or family or organization with self-control is more likely to succeed.

The way to gain control is to set a standard and stick to it firmly.

If you're a boss or a parent, think hard about the standards you set and make sure you set those standards carefully. Once you've announced the standard and the penalty for deviating from it, hold to your promise without flinching, and you will have gained a new level of control. You will have derived order from chaos. The method allows your child or your employee to learn self-control and by doing so, you increase the amount of successful action.

When he was first put in charge of a regiment, General Grant found chaos and disorder. The men were dressed slovenly, they showed up late and there was rank insubordination.

Before you can accomplish something, you first have to establish order, and that's what Grant did. When someone showed up late for roll-call, the whole regiment went without food for twenty-four hours. A man was tied to a post all day if he disobeyed orders. When a soldier cussed, he was gagged.

Rules were established, cleanliness was created, and order was the name of the game. They could get on with the task of training and fighting. Then Grant took these same men and captured Fort Donelson and *fifteen thousand* prisoners in one afternoon! That victory turned the tide for the Union forces.

Discipline is difficult. Our yearning for freedom bucks against it. But without discipline, little can be accomplished. It's a simple fact: Ultimately, it's more difficult and painful to do *without* discipline than it is to buckle down and establish control.

Set standards and stick to them through storm and thunder. You will derive gain from the pain. Success will be your sweet reward.

Set standards and stick to them.

The Samurai Effect

YEARS AGO I READ THE BOOK *Shogun,* by James Clavell, about the Japanese samurai (professional warriors). A samurai gave total allegiance to his liege lord and would die for him without question. The whole system was filled with honor and loyalty and was very beautiful in that respect.

While reading the book, I started treating my boss like my liege lord. What a difference it made! My attitude toward my boss changed *and my boss's attitude toward me changed dramatically*. The working relationship became smoother, more friendly and more efficient. I did everything my boss asked me to do, to the best of my ability and without question. Of course, if my boss asked me to jump off a bridge, I wouldn't have, but usually bosses don't ask employees to do anything but their jobs.

I've often seen a different kind of attitude in the workplace, however, and I'm sure you've seen it too. It can be stated as "I'm not going to kiss anyone's ass!" This attitude is characterized by arguing with the boss when asked to do something or trying to get away with not doing it very well. These people, even more than the rest of us, don't like being told what to do, and actively resist it, which forces the boss to bear down to maintain control, turning the working relationship into an unnecessarily antagonistic contest of wills.

I've worked with people who got along great with everyone *except the boss.* And I've worked in places where *I* had a great boss, but my coworkers had a supreme jerk for a boss—*and it was the same person.* My "samurai" attitude had changed my boss for me.

In a way, your attitude toward a person *creates* that person. Interact with someone with a chip on your shoulder and the person will usually respond defensively. Approach someone with friendliness and cooperation and the person is likely to respond in kind. We play a part in creating the way someone treats us.

Do you want to stand out? Treat your boss like a liege lord and do what she or he asks you to do—cheerfully, without question, and to the best of your ability—and you will stand out. In your boss's mind, you will contrast sharply with the people who don't want to be told what to do. And it'll be more enjoyable for you to be at work.

Create a boss you enjoy working with. In actual behavior, the difference isn't much. You won't be any more tired or worn out by it. But you and your organization will be better off when you adopt a samurai attitude.

Treat your boss like a liege lord.

Try not to become a man of success but rather try to become a man of value.

— *Albert Einstein*

Experience shows that success is due less to ability than to zeal. The winner is he who gives himself to his work, body and soul.

— *Baxton*

Unnatural Acts

HAVE YOU EVER WONDERED why your coworkers complain so much? Or why you find fault with people so easily? Or why you watch the news even though it's depressing? Why?

Our species evolved during the Ice Age (the Pleistocene epoch). In the last one or two million years, there have been four glaciations—four times when the ice advanced southward for a hundred thousand years or so, and then receded, changing the climate dramatically again and again. These ice invasions caused the extinction of many animals. But not humans. Our species lived through the harsh and radically-changing weather, famines, floods, fires, plagues, and the threat of deadly carnivorous animals walking around hungry. Lots of people died. Natural selection had a field day.

Let's speculate for a moment. During dangerous times, what kind of human do you suppose would evolve? Would a happy-go-lucky, everything-is-groovy attitude help one survive? I don't think so. Under those conditions, the best survivors would be those who compulsively noticed what was wrong and were constantly on the lookout for possible danger. In other words, conditions would have selected for a critical, negative, worry-wort. A relaxed, easygoing positive thinker probably wouldn't last one winter. Those people who survived are our ancestors, so those traits are built into our brains and hormonal systems. Even yours.

It is completely natural to notice what's wrong, what doesn't work, and what you don't like. It's somewhat unnatural to see what's good, what's going well, and what you like and appreciate. But it's also unnatural to be toilet-trained. It's unnatural to have good manners. It's unnatural to delay gratification. What comes naturally (like being negative) is not necessarily best. It might have been absolutely essential for survival a hundred thousand years ago, but times have changed.

Luckily, we are capable of doing things we don't naturally do—if we know it's in our best interest and if we firmly and definitely make up our minds to do so. One of the greatest talents of our species is that we're capable of doing what we don't naturally do.

You can learn to notice what's going well. It takes a deliberate, conscious effort. It'll probably never come naturally (that is, without thinking about it). No matter how many years you make that conscious effort, whenever you look around, chances are the first thing you'll see is what's wrong. And that's perfectly okay. It's useful to be able to see what needs fixing. But it also helps to notice the good stuff.

Today, deliberately notice something you like about the company you work for and tell somebody. Then take a good look at your coworkers and find something you honestly appreciate about someone and tell that person you appreciate it. Then talk about someone behind her back—talk about what you admire and respect about her. Make this effort a couple of times a day and your relationships will work better. You'll also be in a good mood more often.

Set a goal at the beginning of the day. How many sincere acknowledgments will you give today? Don't make your goal too big—you have work to do too. But create some way of keeping track. For example, you could put five pennies in your left pocket and every time you make a good acknowledgment, move one penny to your right pocket. Try to move all of them that day.

Make a regular practice of this and the atmosphere where you work will change. The people around you will feel more noticed and appreciated and liked. And they will treat you with more appreciation in return. All you need to do is commit some unnatural acts.

Notice something you appreciate and tell someone.

The Shortest Distance

WHEN IT COMES TO SOLVING problems, using a formal procedure works better than letting your mind wander, so I have one for you. It involves four steps, and you do them in order. These steps are ancient. You could almost say this is *the* method to solve a problem. Anything else is less efficient and less effective. When you look them over you may think this is all very obvious and you can easily see why this method will work. But the important thing is *using* it. When you are confronting a problem, *use* this method:

1. **Clarify the problem.** Attempt to write down what the problem is, specifically. Writing it down is better than doing it in your head. Use a lot of paper on this one; it's an important process. Write something down, then try to improve on it. Keep working until you have a clear, simple statement of the problem.

2. **List the causes.** What has caused this problem? Usually a problem has more than one cause. List them all.

3. **Create possible solutions**. This is where you can use your imagination. During this stage, first come up with all the ideas you can think of. Then kick back and relax. Use your imagination. Let your mind ponder the problem in its own way, as if you were daydreaming about possible solutions. Look at it from different perspectives. How would an old sea captain look at this problem? How would Gandhi look at this problem? You don't know how those people would *actually* look at the problem. But you can use your imagination and that will get you out of your habitual point of view. Let your mind wander, but keep bringing it back to the problem. Don't work at it. Do it in a way that is playful and fun. And stop every once in a while and jot down some ideas.

4. **Select your favorite solution and try it**. You have a collection of possible solutions, and reading through them probably sparked some more ideas. Write them all down. Then look over your ideas and choose what you think is the finest solution among them. Now put it into action.

YOUR SOLUTION WON'T always work. No big deal if it doesn't—you have others to try. Take this step-by-step approach and you'll gain traction and equilibrium and a feeling of control—something that really helps when you've got a problem to deal with.

Problems are an important part of life, and it's always in your best interest to improve your ability to create good solutions. Mastering this formal procedure will help. It may be the shortest distance between a problem and a satisfying solution.

To solve a problem:
Define the problem, list the causes, think up possible solutions, and pick the best one.

Most people think once or twice during their lives. I have become rich and famous by thinking once or twice a week!

— George Bernard Shaw

American Reading Ceremony

HAVE YOU EVER WATCHED a Japanese Tea Ceremony? It's really nothing special except for one thing. The person performing the ceremony is paying attention. But that one thing makes it extraordinary for both the observers and the performer herself.

Something simple takes place. Someone makes tea and then someone drinks it. But the spirit in which it is done makes the difference. Everybody present is paying attention and not doing anything else. The person making the tea moves deliberately, unhurried, trying to make each movement perfect.

There's nothing special about tea. Anyone can do the same thing *doing just about anything*. You can have an American Lunch Ceremony—eat your lunch deliberately, paying attention to what you're doing, unhurried, trying to make each movement in complete awareness.

Try it sometimes when you feel stressed. You can even do it while you work (American Work Ceremony). If you have no immediate deadline, do your work for ten minutes carefully, with full attention on every move, slowly and deliberately. It's a nice little change of pace, if nothing else. But usually there *is* something else, and that's why the Japanese Zen Masters consider the Tea Ceremony as a high art and a worthy practice.

The deliberate movement clarifies your mind and sometimes puts you in a state of tranquillity. It often makes you aware that this moment is all there is and all that needs to be. It's hard to describe, but you don't need a description. Try it and experience it for yourself. It's nothing mystical. If anything, it is a more down-to-earth experience than our usual hustle and bustle because all you're doing is paying attention to what you're doing. Rather than thinking about yesterday's golf game or tonight's dinner, rather than worrying about something that might happen tomorrow or fuming about what happened this morning, rather than wishing you were somewhere else or hoping things change in your future, you're just here, now, doing what you're doing. It is surprising how seldom we do that.

You can do it anywhere, any time. Try it right now while you're reading. Notice your posture, the sounds in the room, the smells, without trying to change anything. Notice your feelings—your emotional tone, the sensations in your stomach, the feeling of your hands and your forehead...notice the page, the feel of your eyes as they move along the line, the voice in your head saying these words. Just notice.

Thank you for participating with me in this American Reading Ceremony.

**Slow down your movements
once in awhile and pay attention.**

---

*Normally we do not so much look at things
as overlook them.*

— Alan Watts

*[Many people have] equated the attainment
of happiness with the relentless pursuit of a
particular path, whether it is looking just right,
being successful, or having it all. They possess
the basic human need for peace of mind, but
they pursue goals that never lead to it.*

— Melvin Kinder

Work Is Good Therapy

THERAPY CAN BE EXPENSIVE. Work is cheap—they even *pay* you for it! When your work is challenging enough to fully compel your attention, but not so challenging it outstrips your ability, you enter The Enjoyment Zone, where your attention is focussed on what you're doing, where you're experiencing the pleasure of being engrossed and engaged in what you're doing, where the petty worries and frustrations that normally plague your mind have no foothold. And whether or not you work in The Enjoyment Zone is up to you, not the job. You can *make* your job into an enjoyable pursuit.

If you want to read more about that, read Mihaly Csikszentmihalyi's excellent book, *Flow: The Psychology of Optimal Experience.*

When you can work in that enjoyable state of concentration, you're giving yourself an excellent form of therapy. Work can be therapeutic! It can heal and restore your mind. It can rid you of depression, negative moods, and feelings of helplessness. And it can give you confidence and self-esteem.

One of the things that contributes to negative, unpleasant emotions is *rumination*: dwelling on thoughts you can do nothing about, running negative and self-defeating thoughts through your head over and over, convincing yourself ever more thoroughly of the validity of your misery. Once these kinds of thoughts get going, they're hard to stop. You feel bad, you think about your situation in a negative way because you feel bad, and then the negative way you're thinking just makes you feel worse. The thoughts aren't doing you any good. The best thing you can do is stop thinking about it, but you can't seem to do that. You're like a train on a track, and there's nowhere to go but down.

Engaging work takes your mind off that track. Like distracting a crying baby with a rattle, your mind gets sent in a new direction.

And while you're working, you're *causing an effect*. Even moving your fingers on a keyboard causes an effect. Helplessness is a core symptom of depression, contributing to it and often causing it. Productive work proves you are *not* helpless, so simply doing your work can lessen or even eliminate a bout of depression.

Also, when you work in The Enjoyment Zone, your skills improve. One inevitable consequence of challenging work is an increase in competence and expertise. This gives you confidence and self-esteem—not based merely on the encouraging words of a therapist, but based on real evidence.

Work cannot accomplish everything therapy can, but it can do a great deal of therapeutic good—far more good than leisure (most leisure produces nothing: it doesn't increase skills, competence or self-esteem, and it doesn't engage your mind enough to stop ruminations). Work has, however, been an effective therapy for generations of people. And it can work as well for you.

To get your mind off your troubles
and increase your feelings of self-worth:
Get to work—keep it challenging,
but not stressful.

The true fruits of successful living are not
material. They are contentment, the joy
of usefulness, growth through the fulfillment
of our particular talent.

— Conrad Hilton

Work Principles

**If you're bored, increase your challenge.
If you're stressed, increase your skill.**

Make a list and put it in order.

Vividly imagine the *completion* of important tasks.

**Whatever happens, use it
to accomplish your purpose.**

Rather than give up:
**Get help, tackle the obstacles one at a time,
and get some training.**

Keep your word.

Assume extra effort is an investment that
returns to you with compound interest.

Increase your ability to get along with people
and improve your disposition.

To earn more respect:
Increase your competence, use good manners,
and speak up rather than smolder.

During a dull task, move faster
or listen to something.

Find something you like to do that is needed
and wanted. Put more of it in your life.

Listen to your own heart.
Don't let your music die with you.

Just keep planting.

When you notice your mind has wandered,
bring it back to the task at hand.

Act more energetic.

Use your own energy during your leisure time.

To earn more money:
Increase your service, and continue to learn about your work, good health, and people.

To handle a troublemaker at work:
Do your work exceptionally well, keep your integrity level high, and stay in good communication with everyone else.

Learn to like competition and compete with honor.

Find a purpose you're enthusiastic about and get to it.

Decide how you want to act, and act that way.

Replace some of your TV time with game playing.

Ask yourself, "What can I take credit for?"

**Think about what you want
and try to make it happen.**

Forbid something for the day.

**Notice when you're drifting away from your *own*
purposes, and then get back on track.**

To increase your vocabulary:
**Look up words, listen to vocabulary tapes,
and use vocabulary flash cards.**

**Get so engrossed in your work
that you forget about everything else.**

Make your life better by reading helpful books.

To read faster and increase your comprehension:
**Don't let your eyes regress, practice picking up
speed, and take in more words at a time.**

When you're working, try to burn calories.

Set standards and stick to them.

Treat your boss like a liege lord.

Notice something you appreciate and tell someone.

To solve a problem:
**Define the problem, list the causes,
think up possible solutions, and pick the best one.**

**Slow down your movements
once in awhile and pay attention.**

*To get your mind off your troubles
and increase your feelings of self-worth:*
Get to work—keep it challenging, but not stressful.

People

How to Avoid Feeling Socially Awkward

WE'VE ALL FELT IT. You don't know what to say or what to do. You feel too aware of yourself and how you're standing, how you're looking, what you sound like. If you have teenagers, you know they feel it intensely. And some of the things teens do that seem so incomprehensible to parents stem from a simple desire to avoid feeling socially awkward.

Although it's very natural to feel awkward around people you don't know very well, it isn't pleasant or productive. Here are two practical things anyone can do to feel more socially comfortable:

1. **Relax your muscles.** This makes you calmer. Most people don't have any problem at all being social around people when they're relaxed. That's why social gatherings have traditionally served alcoholic beverages: It relaxes people. Find a muscle in your body that feels a little tense and consciously relax that muscle. You will instantly feel more at ease.

2. **Make it your mission to help *the other* person feel more comfortable.** Make conversation easy *for the other person* by asking questions she'll enjoy answering. Find out the person's name, whether she's from this area, or if she's not, where she's from. Her answers will probably stimulate other questions and conversation. How about her family: Do they live in this area? Big family? Brothers and sisters? What do they do? How about work? What does she do for a living? Does she like it? What got her into it? How about travel? What parts of the world has she seen? Any hobbies? Listen with interest. Let her know you like what she's saying. Help *her* feel comfortable.

THAT IS BASICALLY six areas to talk about: name, home, family, work, travel, hobbies. Memorize that list of six topics, and when the time comes, the questions will come to mind easily, keeping the conversation lively and smooth. A smooth and lively conversation will put the other person at ease which will make you feel more comfortable. You'll probably never get to all six of the topics because as the other person starts talking, you'll find points of interest you'll want to know more about, and the two of you will start talking about that, and off you'll go into Conversation Land. You'll get to know the person and have a wonderful time and you'll just forget to feel awkward because you can only feel awkward when you're self-conscious. As you become increasingly conscious of the other person, you become less conscious of yourself and your awkwardness disappears.

Relieve your social awkwardness by relaxing and concerning yourself with helping the *other* person feel comfortable. People will love you for it.

Relax your muscles and make it your mission to help the *other* person feel more comfortable.

He who wishes to secure the good of others has already secured his own.

— Confucius

Your Inner Guide to Self-Esteem

SELF-ESTEEM HAS BEEN A HOT TOPIC for years. And for a good reason: Low self-esteem is a source of trouble—bad marriages, social isolation, violence, lack of success, depression, conflict in the workplace, etc. Low self-esteem causes problems. The obvious solution is to try to improve people's self-esteem by pointing out their good traits. Psychologists told us we could give our children high self-esteem by complimenting and praising them often. And they said you could protect yourself by making an effort to think well of yourself—say good things to yourself, repeat affirmations, acknowledge your good traits, etc.

Recent research at Wake Forest University might be turning that popular philosophy completely upside down. The funny thing is, when all the smoke has cleared, what we have left bears a remarkable resemblance to simple common sense.

According to the research, self-esteem appears to be an internal guide to how well we're doing socially, somewhat like our internal guide to the temperature.

When you feel hot, you take off some clothing or open a window. When you feel cold, you bundle up. Although you might be able to repeat to yourself over and over "I feel warm, I feel warm," there are better things to do with your time. Might as well just put on a sweater and get on with it. It's useful to have an internal guide— a feeling—that lets you know what's happening in the world around you, and gives you some motivation to do something about it.

Apparently, that's exactly what self-esteem is.

The feeling of low self-esteem is apparently nothing more than an indication you aren't getting enough positive feedback from other people. You may not be getting rejected or criticized, but to really feel good about ourselves, we need something more than that. We need acknowledgment, compliments, appreciation. We need people to notice us and like us.

This is where it gets tricky. As a parent, you might want to improve your child's self-esteem by giving him lots of compliments. But watch out. If you exaggerate your acknowledgments or if you sometimes make a big deal out of a small thing or resort to puffery, you may be setting your child's internal gauge "off the beam." You've set his social-status meter too high, and it no longer measures the situation accurately. Your child then grows up and goes out into the world and has difficulty dealing with people.

Some new research at Northeastern University showed that people who think well of themselves *regardless of how others feel about them* tend to be perceived by others as condescending and hostile.

Given this new information, a different approach to creating self-esteem seems in order: Giving honest and *accurate* feedback to our children, our spouses, and our employees. It's relatively easy to compliment and praise people. It makes them feel good, and it makes *us* feel good to make *them* feel good. It's more difficult to find something you *genuinely* appreciate and to say it without the slightest bit of puffery, but it just might do more good.

We can also help people *do* better. Of course! If someone is getting along well with her peers and she's succeeding at something—trumpet, hobby, schoolwork, job, athletics—it will improve her self-esteem. So find a way to help her accomplish something. When people *do* well, they tend to *feel better* about themselves.

When you want to build *your own* self-esteem, it appears your best bet is to change your behavior. Do your tasks *well* and treat people *well* and you'll feel good about yourself. Don't worry so much about how you think about yourself. Change what you *do* to make yourself more appreciated by the people around you. Increase your value to other people and to the company you work for. Watch the reactions of other people. Pay attention to the reality outside your skin. Do more of what works. Do less of what doesn't get the response you want. Your self-esteem, your internal "sociometer" will rise as an accurate reflection of your true abilities and where you stand with the people in your life.

To improve the self-esteem of others:
**Give unexaggerated feedback
and help them gain ability.**

To improve your own self-esteem:
**Change what you *do* to make yourself
more appreciated by the people around you.**

Truth is a deep kindness.
— Kahlil Gibran

*...contrary to popular wisdom, increasing
children's self-esteem is not always a good
idea—especially if it is achieved by lowering
their expectations.*

— Mihaly Csikszentmihalyi

Complaint Compunctions

YOU'VE HEARD PEOPLE COMPLAIN. Everybody does it at least some of the time, and many people do it a lot. A person who is complaining usually thinks he is perfectly justified because *everybody knows* how healthy it is to express one's anger (or annoyance or disgruntlement). It's called "venting." It is a very common and widespread belief that venting is healthy. But psychological research has shown that the expression of anger actually makes people angrier. The idea that somehow people store up anger in their bodies that then needs to be released is an inaccurate theory. It is a "common sense" idea based on a Freudian theory and seemingly backed up by the everyday observation that some things *do* seem to get rid of anger: exercise and airing grievances. And it's true. Airing a grievance makes anger disappear. But complaining does not.

"But," you might be saying, "isn't airing a grievance and complaining the same thing?" The answer is that they are *almost* the same thing. The only difference is *who* you're talking to. If you have a grievance with George and you tell it to *me*, you are complaining and it won't help to dissipate your anger. In fact, it has a very good chance of making your anger *worse*. But if you tell your grievance to *George*, your anger or feelings of annoyance are likely to vanish.

If the person who is "venting" really wants to feel better, he needs to communicate with a person who can do something about his complaint.

Therefore, I heartily recommend that you instigate this as your personal policy: *All complaints should go to the person who can do something about it.* That means when someone is complaining to you about someone else, you can kindly direct them to the person who can do something about it. This may seem a rather rough thing to do, and you can surely be as courteous and friendly about it as you are able, but it is the most sane and productive way to deal with those complaints. And if *you* have a complaint, turn it into a request and then talk to the person who can fulfill that request.

ALL COMPLAINTS SHOULD GO TO THE PERSON WHO CAN DO SOMETHING ABOUT IT.

Write that statement on a card and hang it on the wall. Post it at work. Memorize it. Print it on business cards to hand to people who complain to you. Tattoo it on your back. Perhaps I'm getting carried away.

But I'll tell you why that statement makes a good personal policy. If you have to listen to Alice complaining about Sam, you are forced by social pressure to side with Alice against Sam, sympathizing with her. This will weaken your relationship with Sam (or make you two-faced). Another option you have is to defend Sam, thereby perhaps straining your relationship with Alice.

A third alternative is to say, "I think Sam is the one you ought to be talking to about this."

People will naturally complain to someone who isn't involved because it's *easier* than complaining to someone who can do something about it. But it doesn't improve anything.

If the complaint isn't important enough to take it to someone who can do something about it, then it isn't important enough to bother *you* with, either. If it *is* important, it should probably be said—to the person who can do something about it.

This simple policy can take a negative, unproductive expression and turn it into a force for positive change.

**Direct all complaints to the person
who can do something about it.**

Here Comes the Judge

YOU ARE KIND AND GENEROUS most of the time. But occasionally you judge, label and disapprove of people—sometimes silently in your mind, sometimes aloud, sometimes for significant reasons, sometimes for petty reasons. Judging people causes an underlying resentment that puts you in a bad mood and makes you tired. And it strains your relationships with people. The stresses from different sources in your life accumulate, and this is a source you can do without.

And no matter how you do it or what the circumstances, when you pass judgement on someone, you are very likely making an error—usually committing at least one of these three forms of what cognitive scientists call *distorted thinking*:

1. **Jumping to conclusions.** We rarely know the motives or full story behind the actions a person takes, and yet we come to conclusions quickly and easily that "he's a jerk" or "she's a fool" or "how rude" or "what a freak." We condemn people far too easily.

2. **Overgeneralization.** A judgment normally involves summing up a complex human being in simple terms based on a few or even one instance. That's poor science and faulty thinking.

3. **Overconfidence in one's own assessment.** You don't really know why other people do things. And yet you hold your judgments with excessive confidence. We all do it. Overconfidence in our conclusions is a fallibility of human nature.

THESE THOUGHT-MISTAKES can be corrected with practice. The technique is simple: Pay attention to your assessments of other people, and then question and criticize your judgments. Are you jumping to conclusions? Are you overgeneralizing? Do you have enough knowledge to be able to make such an assessment?

Think about it rationally. Maybe you're being too hasty. Maybe you're being unnecessarily harsh. Haven't you yourself done something similar? Sure you have. *But there were extenuating circumstances* that at least partially excused you, weren't there? Maybe this person has reasons too, but you don't know about them. It's not only possible, it's very likely.

Question your judgments and you'll find that many of them aren't worth much, and you'll stop holding them.

And what will happen? You'll feel less stress. You'll find your relationships gently blossoming in a new way. You'll be able to talk to the person more freely. You'll be more relaxed. Conflicts will be easier to resolve because you'll be able to communicate without anger (no judgement, no anger) and without making the other person defensive (when you're not judging, people don't feel attacked, so they don't get defensive). And in the long run, less stress, anger, and frustration adds up to better health too.

Once you start paying attention to it, you may find out you're in the habit of judging people a lot. Does this make you bad and wrong? No. Only human. Judging *yourself* is faulty thinking too.

Question and criticize your negative judgements of people.

---

*If we could read the secret history of
our enemies, we should find in each man's
life sorrow and suffering enough
to disarm all hostility.*

— Henry Wadsworth Longfellow

The Power
of Listening

WHAT IF WE *REALLY* LISTENED to people, instead of do-ing what passes for listening most of the time? The person talking to you would have an extraordinary experience. With your observational powers on full throttle, you'd perceive more than you normally do, and your speaker would feel that something uncommon was taking place. Not only would you understand the speaker's words, but you'd grasp her small nuances of meaning. You'd perceive how she feels about you. You'd understand more of her personality. And you'd probably know something of what she's leaving *un*said as well.

  The difference between you (fully listening) and other listeners (with minds wandering) would be so noticeable as to be startling.

Why is this important? Because your overall effectiveness in life depends on your ability to deal with people well. This discipline of listening will send your ability with people into another league entirely!

A man once said of Sigmund Freud, "He struck me so forcibly that I shall never forget him. His eyes were mild and genial. His voice was low and kind. His gestures were few. But the attention he gave me, his appreciation of what I said, even when I said it badly, was extraordinary. *You've no idea what it meant to be listened to like that.*"

Fully concentrating your attention on the speaker is only the beginning of better listening. It's a necessary first step, like the undercoat of a painting, but it's only the start.

To be a first-class listener, you'd encourage the speaker, you'd let her know with your nods and expressions and body language that you appreciate what she's saying, that you enjoy the conversation, and most of all, that you respect her.

When you listen this way, you won't be silent. You won't be passive. On the contrary, you'll be *exerting* yourself because you need to be doing several things simultaneously: You're taking in the information; you're picking up on the emotional significance being communicated; you're letting the speaker know that you understand and appreciate what she's saying—and you're doing all this without interrupting her flow of speech.

Also, when you're listening well, you're asking the person questions that she'll enjoy answering or questions that she'll find valuable to answer; you're helping her clarify what she's saying so she's left with more understanding about herself after she's done talking with you; and you're communicating silently to the speaker that you respect what she's saying, even when you disagree.

When you *do* disagree, learn to avoid making a direct assertion that disagrees or invalidates her ideas. Instead, learn to say, "I feel that such and such is the case. I may be wrong but I got my information in this magazine (or wherever you got it)."

This is a lot to do simultaneously. It's not easy. It's a discipline. Treat it like any other difficult skill and practice, practice, practice. The benefits to the person speaking are the satisfaction of being heard and understood. The person gets the joy of intimacy, a feeling of closeness, and the rare experience of talking with someone who really cares.

And what about you? You'll become a better person by practicing this discipline—you'll grow stronger and more perceptive. You'll improve your ability to concentrate. You relationships will be more strongly bonded. You'll understand more about the people in your life.

So practice listening. It will teach you about yourself and other people, and you'll win loyal allies and lifelong friends.

As a personal discipline, practice listening well when someone is talking to you.

Confidence With People

WITH CONFIDENCE YOU'RE MORE ATTRACTIVE and likable, and you feel better than when you *lack* confidence. You've experienced the truth of that statement many times in your life. But isn't confidence something you either have or don't, something you're either born with or not? Can you deliberately *become* confident?

I'm confident you can.

You see, if we just use a synonym for confident, the way becomes obvious. One of its synonyms is "certain." And it is true that you feel confident wherever you have a lot of certainty. Think about it. For a teenage boy who wants to talk to a girl he likes, he may feel very awkward and not confident at all. But if he knew a lot about computers, and she was having a problem with a computer and asked his help, he could help her and feel confident doing so. Why? Because he would know what he was talking about. People feel confident when they are certain.

Therefore, wherever you would like to feel confident, develop more certainty about it. And I don't mean an *attitude* of certainty, I mean to develop real honest-to-goodness, actual certainty.

If, for example, you have to get up and speak to a group next week and you don't feel confident about it, start working to develop some degree of certainty: Talk to the people you need to talk to and find out who will be there and what they are expecting, and then prepare thoroughly. The more you prepare, rehearse, talk about what you will say to your friends, make notes, do research, the more certain you will be and the more confident you will feel.

As another example, a shy person might feel a lack of confidence meeting new people. When she's introduced, she feels like running away. This is very common. Why? Because a new person is—by definition—unknown. Our shy person is not certain about anything except the person's name (and if she is too distracted by her nervousness, she'll quickly lose her certainty about that too).

But surprisingly, even with a person you've never met before, you can know with certainty quite a bit about him. And our shy person can increase her certainty and therefore her confidence when dealing with people by:

> 1. Learning more about the human nature we all have in common.

> 2. Learning more about manners (so you're certain about what should be done when).

> 3. Learning strategies for getting to know someone.

YOU CAN LEARN human nature and manners and strategies so well you have a high degree of certainty about those things. This would add up to more confidence around people—even people you've never met before. A good book to start with is Dale Carnegie's *How to Win Friends and Influence People.*

But there are many ways to gain certainty about people, and each one increases your feeling of confidence a little more. Confidence is not on or off; there are many shades of gray from No Confidence to Absolute Confidence. Any actions you take to increase your level of certainty slides you over a little more toward Absolute Confidence.

Increase your certainty about how to act.

Attitudes and Kin

OUR MOODS HAVE A SIGNIFICANT IMPACT on our health
and our ability to make sound decisions. When something consistently alters your mood for the worse, it's
bad for you. And whatever puts you in a bad mood is bad
for your spouse and kids too, because your moods are
contagious.

The bad moods of many people are often caused by
one of their relatives—Mom, Dad, a brother or sister, an
in-law. The trouble is, we tend to put up with lousy behavior from a relative—behavior we would never tolerate
in our spouse or children or in our friends. We don't speak
up. We feel that we *have* to put up with it because they
are "family." But we don't.

There is no law that says you have to stay on good terms with a person just because he's a relative. You don't. And trying to stay on good terms might bring you down and, by contagion, put your spouse and children in a bad mood often enough to affect their health and their ability to get along with others.

It's only a matter of luck whether your relatives can also be your friends. If you didn't get lucky, don't worry about it. You have your spouse and kids to take care of. And there are plenty of people other than your relatives you can have for friends—people who will treat you well.

Should you write off a relative who brings you down? No. There's a better way. Simply follow these two rules:

1. **Be honest**
2. **Don't judge**

THESE TWO WILL help you clean up a relationship. Those who bring you down will tend to gradually remove themselves voluntarily from your life.

The truth is, when someone is bringing us down regularly, *we are collaborating in the process* by withholding honest statements. For example: "Would you please call me later? I'm busy right now." We don't say stuff like that because we're trying to be polite. We don't want to be rude. But whatever the reason we have for withholding honest communication, hiding the truth only digs us deeper and deeper into the mess.

The way out is with straighforward information, such as the following: "I don't really feel we should talk about him behind his back." "That question kind of makes me uncomfortable." "I don't want you to visit." "I think you drink too much and I don't want my kids to be around it." Simple, honest communication is all you need.

Some honest statements may seem unnecessarily harsh. But those are the kind of things you need to say sometimes if you want to protect your psychological and physical health and that of your spouse and kids. The problem is we sometimes don't have enough courage to say those things until we are really mad. They seem so harsh, you'd think you'd have to be angry to say them. But you don't. You don't even have to think the person is wrong. In fact, that's the other half it: Restrain yourself from judging the person. If you judge your relative and make him wrong, you hurt him and yourself, and that's unnecessary. You can speak honestly without judgement. It may take some practice, but you can do it. Concentrate on it. Memorize those two rules. Chant them to yourself when you're visiting with the person or talking to them over the phone. Be honest gently, without judgement.

So the way to deal with a relative who puts you in a bad mood is to let him be the way he is while also taking care of yourself by being honest. Remind yourself that if you had similar upbringing and genetics, you might very well be like him, so there's no justification for writing him off as a bad person. You don't know how he came to be that way and you don't know his motives. All you really know is he brings *you* down.

Concern yourself with being honest—without judgment—and the honesty will take care of your situation for you. Your relative will either respond to your honesty well and your relationship will improve, or he won't like your honesty—he won't want to be around you—and he will voluntarily phase *you* out of *his* life. Either way, you're better off. It may be a little rough for awhile, but you and your spouse and your children will come out on the other side healthier and happier.

Clean up relationships by being honest without judgement.

The truth that many people never understand, until it is too late, is that the more you try to avoid suffering the more you suffer because smaller things begin to torture you in proportion to your fear of suffering.

— Thomas Merton

I cannot give you the formula for success, but I can give you the formula for failure: try to please everyone.

— Herbert Bayard Swope

Very Impressive

I REMEMBER READING about an ingenious experiment on how hard it is to change people's minds after they've already formed an opinion. The researchers took people who believed in the death penalty and people who didn't, and showed them studies on the subject. Some studies were comparisons between two states of the U.S., one with the death penalty and one without, and how their crime rate differed. Other studies showed before and after crime rates of states who either did or didn't have the death penalty and then changed.

The experimenters discovered that no matter which of the studies they showed people, *their opinions did not change!* Not only that, but whether they were for or against the death penalty, these people, all of whom viewed the same studies, became even *more* convinced of their original opinion. To *all* of them, the studies only *reinforced* their already existing opinions. What they did was find flaws—legitimate in most cases—in the studies, which gave them a good reason not to change their opinion. But they only criticized the study that did *not* support their opinion and they praised the study that *did*, pointing out all the (again, legitimate) reasons the study was a good one. But nobody changed their opinion.

This probably doesn't surprise you. Most of us realize that people don't like to change their opinions, and that they skew their perception of the events of the world to support their own opinions, and tend to criticize or be skeptical of unsupportive events.

Now here's the point: People also do that with their opinions of *you*. When you first meet someone, they size you up and form an opinion about you. If you are cranky the first time you meet someone, they will tend to think of you as a grumpy person. If you are *not* grumpy the next time they see you, they usually won't think to themselves, "Oh, I was mistaken." No. They will think to themselves, "Oh, Mister Grumpy must have gotten some exceptionally good news today." They will discount it if it is inconsistent with their first impression of you.

That's why it often takes a long time to change someone's first impression—and why it's important to make a good one when you have a chance.

Try to make a good first impression.

Make Your Own Labels

THE FOLLOWING EXPERIMENT took place in Brooklyn: sixty-two teenagers were assembled in a room. Labels an inch and a half high were stuck at random on each person's forehead. The labels were all different, saying things like: "Lazy," "Ugly," "Famous," "Rich," "Cool," "Clumsy," "Wimpy," etc. Each person could see everyone elses' label but his or her own, and it was against the rules to tell someone what their label said. They were told to treat each other according to the label on their foreheads. Then they mingled.

At the end of the experiment, one young man said, "I feel distrusted, like I'm some kind of thief. I don't like it." The label on his forehead read, "Dishonest." As you might expect, the people wearing the labels "Rich" and "Famous" enjoyed the way people treated them. The participants could tell, just by the way people treated them, what their label said—maybe not the exact words, but the general idea was pretty clear to each of them.

This illustrates something very useful.

For years self-help authors have implored their readers to change the way they *appear* to others: Dress well, speak with confidence, move with assurance, smile. In other words, act like a well liked, successful person, even if you don't feel like one. Believe it or not, this is practical advice. All these ways of expressing yourself *are like signs on your forehead*. They tell each person you meet, just as surely as if you had it written in big letters, how she or he should treat you. These ways of expressing yourself are signs that say, "I'm successful, well liked, and worthy of respect."

No matter what you do or how you act, you are telling people how they should treat you, and you're conveying that message whether you are trying or not. If the sign on your forehead is a good one, leave it alone. But if you're not getting the response from people you want, make a new label.

Act like a person who is well liked and worthy of respect, even when you don't feel that way.

Danger

I USED TO THINK IT WAS HEALTHY to express anger and unhealthy to hold it in, so I said what was on my mind when I was angry. Of course, I hurt people's feelings—unnecessarily.

Anger can be a dangerous and destructive emotion. Although you can't eliminate the emotion from your life, the way you respond to it can make it less dangerous and more constructive.

Research has shown that expressing anger only makes you angrier. But that doesn't mean we should avoid saying anything about what makes us angry. It's just that we should avoid saying it *while we're angry*. It doesn't do much good anyway: The person listening to you only sees and hears your anger and puts up her defenses right away. Nothing gets through. And she gets a very bad impression of you.

But you need to say something. So follow these two rules and you'll do yourself and other people a big favor:

1. **Make it your personal policy not to say much or decide anything while you're angry.** Leave it alone, go on about your business, and the intensity will subside. *Then* think about what you need to do or say or decide. If you've calmed down and decided to talk to someone but find you can't seem to say it without getting angry again, write it in a letter.

2. **Say what you want, not what you don't want.** Say your complaints in the form of requests. Instead of "You never do such and such," say "Would you please do such and such?" It's easier to hear. It's more likely to cause the effect you want. Say clearly what you want and why you want it.

USUALLY YOU'RE ANGRY because you want someone to change—to do something different than what they're doing. That's perfectly legitimate. What you want is to have an *impact* on the other, which, according to the research, is what will really and truly clear up your anger. Not venting, but not remaining silent either.

Those two steps will help you effectively cause change in other people while reducing the amount of anger you experience over time. Even when you make a request and someone says no, you'll feel better. At least now they know what you want. You've said it. It's off your chest.

This is a good way to increase others' respect for you while also making things go the way you want more often. Turn complaints into requests and make those requests when you are calm.

Don't say much when you're angry.
When you complain, say what you want,
not what you don't want.

I am not naive enough to think that...
you will never fight again in front of
your children. [If it happens, research
shows that you should try to] go out of
your way to resolve the fight...in front
of your child.

— *Martin Seligman*

How to Find
a Lifemate

IN ORDER TO FIND A LOVE FOR LIFE, you'll need to know what your strongest interest is. What really interests you? What do you love to talk about, read about, do, have, play with? If you don't know the answer to those questions, or if the answers are a bunch of minor interests rather than one major interest, forget about finding a mate until you know what your "passion" is. But once you know that, finding a mate is easy: *Pursue your interest and see who shows up.*

Let's say you love sailing. If you want to find someone you'll love to talk to, you'll need to find someone as interested in sailing as you are. Otherwise, although the two of you may have a functional relationship, you'll be living in different worlds. Our deepest purposes and interests are at the heart of who we are.

So join a sailing club, go to sailing classes and races. Pursue your interest. The people you meet in a sailing club are much more likely to be interested in sailing than the people you'd meet in a bar, for example.

The rush of hormones at the beginning of a relationship wears off. Sorry to say it, but it's true. No matter how attractive someone may be, that initial intense rush eventually dies down. But that's okay, because there's a deeper, more satisfying kind of love and attraction: the respect and affection between two people who share a common purpose or interest.

Raising children ends up being the common purpose between many married couples. But if child-raising doesn't intensely interest both of you, it isn't a good enough purpose to create and maintain the longtime happiness of a lifemate.

Two things need to be said. First, *you'll never find the "perfect" mate.* She or he may seem perfect for a while, but no one can meet every one of your ideals. In fact, some of your ideals are probably mutually exclusive, so meeting all of them is literally impossible. You'll eventually find faults in anyone because everyone has faults. When you find faults with your mate, remind yourself of that. Quit imagining that there is a perfect person out there somewhere. There isn't.

Second, even when you've found your lifemate, *you'll sometimes be attracted to others.* It's human. It doesn't mean anything except that you are a biological machine, built to breed. The human species (and every other species on the planet) has a built-in urge to multiply. Stick with your mate and don't let it be important that others attract you. Your response to yourself can simply be "So what if I'm attracted to someone? It doesn't mean anything." Stay true to your mate even when an occasional attraction inclines you temporarily to do otherwise. You'll be happier and healthier as a result.

You want to find a lifemate? Take up your strongest interest with enthusiasm and see who shows up. After you find the person you're looking for and the rush of hormones has worn off, accept the fact that your mate isn't perfect, that nobody is perfect, and remind yourself that it isn't important that you are occasionally attracted to others. Do this and you can live (pretty darn) happily ever after.

To find and keep a good mate:
**Pursue your interest and remind yourself:
Nobody's perfect and attraction
to others is unimportant.**

---

*I think that's what the good life is:
pursuing something that matters to you
alongside someone who matters to you.*

— *J. Klassy Evans*

Personal Propaganda

WHEN THE EXPERTS WANT TO CHANGE the way people think, they use slogans. Why?

Because it works.

Since early in this century, observers have pointed out that in nondemocratic countries, propaganda campaigns have had the tendency to use short, easy-to-remember phrases that encapsulate and symbolize their message. These brief phrases are then repeated over and over again until their meaning becomes part of the thinking habits of the population.

Advertisers do the same thing—*It's the real thing, Just do it, Your true voice, I like what you do for me, Like a rock*—short, pithy, memorable phrases take advantage of the way the human mind works naturally. It's practical. The short phrases focus the mind, simplify the issue and stimulate action.

Our minds don't handle complicated formulas or doctrines very well unless we concentrate our attention. That's fine when we're reading or listening to a lecture. But when it comes down to our daily experiences—when we're late for work, the kids are crying, and we're trying to remember where we left the car keys—we find it distinctly difficult to concentrate our minds on any complicated concept, no matter how beautiful or perfect the philosophy seemed to be when we read it. In the heat of everyday life, we need to focus on what's happening. We don't have extra attention to spend philosophizing about it. That's true for everyone: rich or poor, genius or average, in free countries and in communist countries. That's just how the human brain works.

When a ruthless dictator uses short phrases to focus ideas and make them easier to act on, it may be bad for the people. But you can use the same tool to produce some *good* for yourself. You, too, can take advantage of the way your mind works.

When there's something you want to change about yourself—some habit, some way you deal with others—think it through and then encapsulate your conclusions into a short, easy-to-remember phrase. Say that phrase to yourself often. Use it to focus your mind. Use it to direct your thoughts. Use it to channel your actions in the direction you want.

The source of most of the habits you want to change are *habits of thought.* Change the thought habits and your behavioral habits change too.

For example, when I feel out of my element or I'm dealing with a task that feels too big for me, I often use the principle from the chapter *Adrift.* I tell myself: "I can handle it." With those four words, I remind myself that others have been through worse and it immediately puts my situation in perspective.

Slogans can really help at times like that—times when you're too busy or too emotional or too overwhelmed to do much thinking about it. Say the slogan to yourself and get right back on track in a good frame of mind without skipping a beat.

Make your own propaganda campaign in your head. Use some of the principles of this book, or encapsulate a change you want or an insight you've had into a short phrase and repeat it often. Encapsulate and repeat. Encapsulate and repeat. It's a practical technique for improving your life.

Encapsulate your insights into short phrases and repeat them often.

No steam or gas drives anything until it is confined. No life ever grows great until it is focused, dedicated, disciplined.

— Harry Emerson Fosdick

Play Yourself Down

WHEN YOU HEAR SOMEONE BRAGGING or thinking they're better than you, what's your first instinct? To take them down a notch? Let them know they're not as great as they think they are? And when someone is humble or playing themselves down, what do you want to do? Build them up, probably. It's human nature.

The problem is, when you do well—even if you *aren't* an egotist or a braggart—some people can get the impression you think you're pretty hot stuff, and they'll try to tear you down. Therefore—and here's the point— *if you get more criticism than you want, play yourself down*. Get to it before they do. If you play yourself down well enough and quick enough, the criticizer may even do a complete turnaround and try to build you up. At least they'll have less desire to tear you down. You've taken the wind out of their sails by playing yourself down.

There are rules to playing yourself down. You can't just go around saying, "I'm a sniveling, worthless puddle of scum sludge." Too obvious. Here are a few pointers:

1. **Never lie.** Not only does lying feel bad, but if the other person knows or suspects you're lying, it reverses the effect you're trying to create.

2. **Don't make a big deal about it.** Don't go on and on about how imperfect you are: It'll sound like you're trying to convince yourself. Just make a brief comment and go on.

3. **Point out something the other person is better at than you.** Often people who make a habit of tearing other people down feel intensely competitive, and it'll help them relax to feel like a winner.

4. **Never mention you're better at something than the other person** unless it's absolutely necessary. This will only be difficult if you yourself are intensely competitive.

5. **When you make a mistake, admit it before anyone else can accuse you.** This is a good thing

to do anyway, but it also helps keep people from trying to tear you down.

IT SOUNDS CONTRADICTORY, but people admire humility—as long as it is humility with class. Follow these guidelines and you'll achieve just that. The end result will be a more peaceful, less contentious, happier life.

Play yourself down.

---

*It is far more impressive when
others discover your good qualities
without your help.*

— *Judith Martin*

*Always acknowledge a fault frankly.
This will throw those in authority off
their guard and give you the opportunity
to commit more.*

— *Mark Twain*

*Most of our faults are more pardonable
than the means we use to conceal them.*

— *Francois de la Rochefoucauld*

The Conflict of Honesty

WE'RE AFRAID TO BE HONEST. I'll admit it, I am too. And we *should* be afraid of it. Honesty can cause conflict—uncomfortable, gut-wrenching, upsetting confrontations with people. We hate those and try to avoid them. One of the main reasons we try to avoid conflict is because *we're not very good at it*. And because we avoid it, we never have a chance to *become* good at it.

Luckily, many people have gone before you. Some of them have risked honesty and gotten good at the conflict it can create, and some of them have even written down what they've learned.

It seems that there are some basic rules you can follow, and with a little practice, you *can* learn to deal with conflict in a way that helps other people and yourself at the same time. Here are the two main rules to follow when you find yourself in conflict with someone:

1. **Listen well.** Interruptions block the flow of communication and prevent progress. Sometimes an interruption jars or upsets the speaker. Give people your attention. Let them finish. Do your best to understand what they're saying. You don't have to agree with what they're saying, but try to understand it from their point of view—try to understand why they think that way. And *let them know* you understand.

2. **Speak only what's strictly true.** This sounds a lot easier than it is. Try it. Try going a day only saying what you know is true. I'm not talking about philosophical, airy-fairy stuff, either; I don't mean getting into a debate about whether or not your chair really exists. I mean, in a practical sense, see if you can go a whole day only saying what you know is true. It's tougher than you'd think, so don't treat this one lightly. During conflict, concentrate on saying only what you know is true.

IMPOSE THESE TWO disciplines on yourself. You will be able to be more honest and you'll have more control over your life. This is no small accomplishment. Honesty sounds kind of corny, but more honesty means more freedom and more personal strength. And no lasting peace can settle in your heart without it.

Be honest. If it causes conflict, listen well and only say what is strictly true.

Between them whom there is hearty truth, there is love.

— Henry David Thoreau

The aim of argument or of discussion should not be victory, but progress.

— Joseph Joubert

A truth is always easier to remember than a lie. Being honest is the easiest way to improve your memory.

— Mike Elgan

E-Squared

A COUPLE OF YEARS AGO, my son and I got into an argument. He got defensive and uppity, I got intrusive and sarcastic. I ended the conversation by slamming his bedroom door behind me.

At times like that, I can feel myself wanting to keep up a wall between me and the other person. I wanted to keep making my son wrong. I wanted to see everything wrong about him.

Then I remembered E-Squared (or E^2). E^2 will increase your impact on the person you're talking to—it'll add a subtle, relaxed quality to your demeanor that will help the *other* person feel at ease in your presence. And you'll like what it does for *you* even more. You become calm and at ease and you get a strong feeling of standing on solid ground. I call it E^2 for *experienced experience.*

As each moment goes by, you and I have an ongoing stream of experience—lots of sights, thoughts, sounds, feelings, smells—but we don't register much of it consciously. And that's fine. Nothing wrong with that for the most part. But sometimes it's pretty useful to register your experience consciously. One of those times is when you feel uncomfortable or when you're upset with someone and you think you're going to lose your cool. Another might be when you're giving a speech and you feel like running away or when you're telling someone something they don't want to hear.

At times like those, pay attention to your physical experience. *Experience* your experience. Feel all the different sensations in your body. When you're feeling powerful emotions, there's a lot to pay attention to; emotions are complex; they move through your body producing physical sensations in many different places in your body, in sequence. Pay attention to those.

And while you're paying attention to your physical sensations, you'll notice certain muscles—in your back, in your face, in your shoulders—have contracted and held the contraction. You'll probably notice lots of sensation in your solar plexus region. Pay attention to everything— your body posture, the expression on your face, the light coming into the room, the sounds around you. Notice your breathing, feel your feet on the floor. Be there.

Simple? Sure. Obvious? Absolutely. It is nothing more than experiencing something that you are already experiencing. What could be easier? But sometimes we don't *want* to experience our experience, and it's times like those you have to do it consciously and deliberately. Otherwise you will tend to *act out* those negative feelings or do something in an attempt to avoid feeling those feelings—something you'll regret later.

So I took a deep breath, relaxed, and for a moment I paid attention to my ongoing experience: I noticed my body posture, the expression on my face, the different sensations in my body, the feel of the air on my skin, etc. Then I went back, a changed man, and talked to my son. Those few moments I took to E^2 altered me. They stopped me from reacting—defending and attacking—and allowed me to start fresh. I went back to his room and apologized for slamming the door and explained myself as best I could. I was completely calm and had no edge in my voice. He listened. He knew he'd made a mistake but I had nailed him so hard, he didn't want to admit it before. We ended the conversation with no hard feelings.

E^2 is an act of will. It's not a thought. It's not a physical action. It's a change of heart. Instead of running, you stand and feel. Instead of wanting to hide, you open yourself up. Instead of cowering inside, you pay attention and relax.

Try it. Try it any time you feel like pulling away or shrinking back. Stand firm. Breath deep. Relax your tensions. And feel.

**Practice E-Squared now and then:
Pay close attention to your ongoing experience.**

How You Measure Up

YOU OFTEN COMPARE YOURSELF to others. We all do. You look at the way people look and sound and move, and you check how you measure up. When you stop at an intersection in your car, you watch people walk across the street and you pass judgment on the person's hairstyle, the way they dress, and so on, and you don't even *try* to do this. It is completely automatic.

You may not be able to stop yourself from doing it. But you can change the *way* you do it.

When you compare yourself to people, you look to see how they're *different* from you. And when you look at another and note your differences, it makes you feel *superior* if the comparison turns out in your favor and *inferior* if it turns out in their favor. When you feel superior, your feelings are communicated subtly through the way your body moves and through your voice tone, and this can make the *other* person feel inferior. All this mental nonsense creates a general feeling of alienation—it affects your attitude and your relationships.

But there's another option. Instead of looking for differences, you can look for *similarities*.

Look and listen to people and notice how they are like you. Our feelings of friendliness toward people are affected by how alike we feel. When you know someone is from your home town or went to your college or is the same religion, you automatically feel more kinship with them. When you look for similarities you increase your feelings of compassion and affection toward that person. Where you once felt bad about yourself from an unfavorable comparison or made the other person feel bad because you found him to be inferior, there will now be good feelings.

Try it the next time you catch yourself judging a person or when someone annoys you. Force yourself to notice your similarities. Recall times when you acted in similar ways. Studies show we tend to think others' bad actions stem from personal motives, yet we tend to think our *own* bad actions are caused by circumstances beyond our control. This causes unnecessary anger between people, which is bad for health and doesn't help relationships much. Actively looking for similarities is the antidote. It's a new habit, so it will take some practice, but the process is enjoyable and the end result is too.

Notice how other people are similar to you.

Send a Blessing

WE NOW HAVE SCIENTIFIC EVIDENCE that prayer may actually work. Researchers in California started out with about 400 patients recovering from heart problems. Half the patients received prayers (from a distance), the other half didn't. Nobody in either group was told there was any praying going on.

According to Dr. Dale Matthews, a professor at Georgetown Medical School, those patients who were the targets of prayer had *half* as many complications and they had a lower rate of congestive heart failure than the patients who were not prayed for.

Could it be? Other experiments show the same thing. In 1988, Randolf Byrd, MD, a cardiologist from the University of California at San Francisco School of Medicine started with 393 patients who had either heart attacks or severe chest pains, or both.

Half were prayed for at a distance, half weren't prayed for at all. Seventeen of those not prayed for (NPF) needed antibiotics, compared to three in the prayed-for (PF) group. Fifteen NPFs needed diuretics, compared with five PFs. Twenty NPFs had congestive heart failure; only eight PFs had it. Fourteen NPFs had cardiopulmonary arrest, compared to three PFs. Thirteen NPFs got pneumonia, compared to three PFs. Twelve NPFs needed mechanical respirators. None of the PFs did.

I'm scientifically oriented and skeptical. I think the scientific method is the best thing going to sift facts from wishful thinking. And here we have scientific evidence, but maybe the studies are flawed or biased in some way. You can find something wrong with just about any study. But what the heck—it might be true! So go ahead and send blessings to your friends. It can't do any harm. Send them a wish for wellness or happiness or good luck or even a specific good event like meeting and falling in love with Mr. or Ms. Right. Whether your particular prayer has a direct effect on your friend or not, it will definitely have an effect on *you*. It feels good to send a blessing to someone even with only a vague hope it may help them.

Do what you can for the people you love. And when your day is done, it couldn't hurt—and might help—to send a blessing too.

Send good wishes to people anytime, anywhere.

Personality Myth

SOME OF THE FIRST ZOOLOGISTS to study chimpanzees expected to find brutish apes and were surprised to see peaceful animals being tender toward each other. Later researchers, expecting to find peaceful animals, were often shocked to see them hunt monkeys and tear them limb from limb, or to see an angry male go on a rampage, sometimes injuring or even killing innocent chimp bystanders, or to see, for the first time ever in a nonhuman species, the chimpanzees engage in war.

The truth is, chimpanzees are capable of a wide range of feelings and behaviors. And that is also true of humans. Like you, for instance. Defending the life of someone close to you, you are capable of extreme brutality. When consoling a child, you're capable of the tenderest care. And everywhere in between.

You don't have a fixed personality. You change all the time. You are different now than you were even earlier today.

Any label you hold onto about yourself—a nice person, an angry person, a strong person—is foolish. It will limit you. The label is limiting, and when you force yourself to act in a way consistent with your label, you are taking something big and complex and trying to fit it into a small, simple container. You have to shave off a whole spectrum of behaviors and feelings you're capable of, some of which would be useful.

It's like being a carpenter but labelling yourself only as "the kind of person who hammers." What do you do when you need to saw something? You could grab a saw and get it done quickly. But if you've limited yourself to hammering, you'll pound away till the sun goes down and your work will look terrible when you're done.

Don't limit yourself. Don't label yourself. You're a human being and you're far more flexible than you think. Don't block yourself from your perception of other aspects of yourself. You're not dominate or submissive, inquisitive or close-minded, strong or sensitive—you're capable of all them. Like a carpenter using a wide range of tools, use your full spectrum of personality where it works best and you will accomplish more, get along better with others, and be happier.

Don't limit yourself by giving yourself a narrow label.

Necessary Conflict

CHILDREN TRY TO TRAIN THEIR PARENTS as much as parents try to train their children. Children want their parents to wait on them hand and foot, to buy them whatever they want, to grant them freedom and privilege, and to think everything they do is wonderful.

If you have children, you know this is true. They want a lot from you. And they use whatever tools they can to attain it: throwing a fit, being cute, whining, wearing down resistance with persistence, lying, trying to use your own rules against you, pitting Mom against Dad, pretending to go along with you in order to gain favor, being "good," trying to make you feel guilty, etc. You're familiar with the techniques. Every kid invents them anew and uses whichever techniques he can get away with.

I've seen parents counter their children's strategies with "That makes Mommy unhappy," as if Mom's happiness is on the child's top-priority list. I'd hate to break the news to a mom who says this, but her happiness is way down there, below cookies and cotton candy. The motivation a child has to please a parent is weak compared to the motivation to gain resources and privilege.

Therefore, if you have a child, you must arrange it so there is a strong motivation to do what you want—something more powerful than "It makes me happy." It's not that your child doesn't care about you. It's that the self-discipline it takes to be fair and sacrifice one's own wishes for the good of someone else and for the long term is *learned.* It's not inborn. So while your child *does* want to please you, he also wants cookies and if he can get them by being nice, he will. If he can get them by screaming, he will.

Now that you're an adult, you know it's important to delay gratification. You know vegetables are better for you than cookies. And you have enough appreciation for long-term consequences that you're willing to sacrifice pleasure in the moment. But your child isn't. So the two of you are going to conflict.

In any conflict, failure to be aware of the goals of the other person puts you at a disadvantage in gaining your own goals. You want to buy them a book. They want more junk (toys). You want them to eat vegetables and protein. They want cookies and ice cream. You want to teach them manners and morals. They want you to go pester someone else. By and large, they are not the slightest bit interested in what you really want to give them.

Your goals are in conflict. That *is* the way it is. You *cannot* make your goals align without compromising your integrity, so *you* must be the one who sets the standards and you must deal out consequences when the standards are violated. Reasoning won't work with someone who hasn't had enough experience to appreciate long-term consequences. So you have to create immediate consequences. And the consequences have to be more of a deterrent than the pleasure your child gets from violating the standard. Knowing you're disappointed usually won't do it. "A good talking to" won't either. You need something sufficiently difficult, inconvenient, or painful to make a child choose wisely: a week without dessert, no TV for three days, extra chores. And it only works when you make sure you follow through and enforce the consequences.

This is an important conflict. The way it turns out makes a difference. It's your adult standards against your child's whims. It's conscience against genetically driven impulse. It's experience against ignorance. Who will win? For your sake and for your child's sake, I hope it's you.

**Accept the natural conflict
between parent and child.**

**Set standards and enforce them
with consequences.**

Suggestive Moves

IF YOU FEEL LIKE YAWNING before you finish this article, go right ahead. You know how satisfying a good yawn can be.

I've just given you a suggestion, and whether you like it or not, it has had an effect on you. Just by suggesting something, you can have an influence on people. You don't have to boss them around or be sly to have an influence. You can merely suggest, which is easier and creates less strain on yourself and other people—less strain than either trying to command or trying to be clever.

Of course, if you're a manager or a parent, you'll have to do your share of commanding. But much of what we want other people to do is not in the "must do" category. Most of it is simply our preference. And changing people to fit our preferences is best done with simple suggestions.

We continually influence one another. Hypnosis practitioners find that we are in a semihypnotic state most of the time—our focus is limited and we are open to suggestion. If this is true, and it seems to be so, you can deliberately make the world around you better by speaking up. Say what you think. Suggest things.

You don't have to be pushy, pompous or sneaky. Just be your honest self. And while not all of your suggestions will have an effect, a surprising number of them will, often without your knowledge or even the knowledge of the other. Sometimes you will find people doing what you suggested but they have forgotten it was your suggestion—they think it was their idea. Whether you get the credit or not, whether some of your suggestions are ignored or not, one thing is certain: You'll get more of what you prefer when you speak up than you will by keeping silent, as long as you speak up in a way that doesn't create resistance.

Suggest something. Give yourself permission to have an effect on people. I know you've got some good ideas in that head of yours. I think you should let them out. But it's only a suggestion.

Influence people by merely suggesting things.

We're Family

IN THE MOVIE *MADE IN AMERICA*, a daughter raids the files at the sperm bank her mother used, and despite her shock in finding out her dad is an infamously slick car salesman, she loves him because he's her dad. Everything is beautiful until they discover it was a mistake. He really wasn't her dad after all.

She loved him *because* she thought he was her dad. Most of us are like that. We have an automatic acceptance of people in our family—even a distant cousin we meet for the first time.

What if we treated *all* people as relatives? If they are older, we can imagine them to be uncles or aunts or great uncles or great aunts. If close to our own age, they could be long lost siblings or cousins. Youngsters could be our nieces and nephews. Love comes naturally when we haven't labeled someone as "other."

It's really not much of a stretch. In truth, we all *are* related in one way or another, probably more closely related than you'd think. According to the experts on genetics, you wouldn't have to go very far back in time to find where your family tree intersects with your friend's or spouse's family tree, or anyone's tree you know. And as you keep going back, the trees cross again and again. We are all, at the very least, distant cousins of one another many times over.

Keep this in mind when you interact with people and the world will feel like a friendlier place.

This doesn't mean you have to become an easy target for con artists. You don't have to turn off your good judgement. But you interact with people every day: the bus driver, the clerk at the store, a neighbor, the people you work with. Think of them as family and you'll feel differently toward them, and that'll make you act differently toward them, which will make *them* act differently toward *you*, and voilà! The world is a friendlier, happier place for real.

Practice it on the next three people you talk to, and you'll see what it's like. In your mind, imagine the person is a relative. You don't have to *do* anything differently. Simply entertain the idea that the person may be related. We all know *intellectually* we're all members of the same human family, but it's nice to *feel* it too.

**When you talk to people,
think of them as relatives.**

Mastery

SOMETHING IS HAPPENING. After an entire generation of parents and teachers have worked hard to improve their children's self-esteem, the level of depression in young people has skyrocketed. And according to Martin Seligman, PhD (a researcher who has spent his lifetime studying depression and ways out of it), the two are intimately linked. In his book, *The Optimistic Child*, Seligman writes, "By emphasizing how a child *feels* at the expense of what the child *does*—mastery, persistence, overcoming frustration and boredom, and meeting challenge—parents and teachers are making this generation of children more vulnerable to depression." And he's got a lot of research to back him up.

There's nothing wrong with trying to improve a child's self-esteem. Feeling good about yourself is healthy and valuable. But the *way* you improve self-esteem makes a big difference. When it is done with compliments, even if children feel better about themselves, they will be more vulnerable to depression when they hit one of life's inevitable setbacks. They may feel good about themselves, but if they are weak and incompetent, life will eventually take them down.

On the other hand, if we try to improve our children's self-esteem by helping them learn to overcome barriers and to persist in the face of frustration, if we help them learn to tolerate discomfort long enough to succeed at something, we've given them real and valuable *abilities*. Their confidence and belief in themselves will be based in *reality*, not merely in what people have told them. It's a confidence that cannot easily be shaken.

This way of building a child's self-esteem is harder on the adult and it's harder on the child—in the short run. It's quicker and easier to just say nice things. But in the long run, a sense of competence will do more for a child than any nice things you could tell them. Actions speak louder than words. The child's own actions and the response they get from the world speak louder than any words, no matter how pretty.

Let's give our children something real: *competence*. And from that competence, they will have a self-confidence that renders them immune to depression. The gift of mastery has no equal.

**Improve children's self-esteem by
helping them become more competent.**

Is That Clear?

"I *TOLD* HIM I NEEDED some of his staff to cover things so we could have our meeting," Ann said, "but did he volunteer anyone? No. And then today at the meeting, the supervisor asked him when he was going to have *his* meeting and he had the *gall* to say, 'As soon as Ann loans me the staff to cover it.' I don't get it!"

She doesn't get it. A lot of people don't get it. That's why I will urge you—for the sake of your sanity and effectiveness—to be overly clear when you talk to people because they tend to *assume* they understand when they don't. It is in your best interest to be *too* thorough when communicating to people. It makes you more effective.

"Don't use the one on the right," you say. "It's being repaired. Only use the one on the left."

"Sure. No problem."

Later...

"That machine didn't work," he tells you.

"Which one did you use?" you ask.

"The one on the right."

"I told you to use the one on the left!"

"No you didn't. Remember? You said I should only use the one on the *right.* That's what you said, I swear!"

People sometimes aren't listening very well. Sometimes they have other things on their minds. Sometimes they think they know what you're going to say already, so they don't really listen. And then there is the memory factor; human memory is certainly not the most reliable thing in the world.

You can save yourself a lot of trouble by simply repeating yourself and then questioning people to make sure they *know* what you said.

Be overly clear with your communication and you will experience less resentment and you'll have fewer problems to deal with later.

How can you be overly clear? By using two simple techniques: 1) repeat yourself, and 2) ask questions to make sure people understand *exactly* what you're saying. Be more clear than you think is necessary and you'll experience less stress and more success.

Be overly clear with people.

To Zip or Not to Zip

MY WIFE, KLASSY, was upset about something. As usual, I was trying to help her fix it, which just annoyed her even more. "You don't listen to me," she said, "You just don't understand how I feel." She had said that to me many times before. I must not have been listening.

Of course, when *I'm* troubled, she listens and I feel better. All of a sudden it occurred to me to find out how she did it. Maybe she had some strategy.

But when I asked her, all she could tell me was, "I just try to see things from your point of view." I'd heard that one before. I pressed her for more detail, and after awhile, she was able to tell me what she did. She had been using a technique without realizing it.

Her method is a lot easier than reading *How to Win Friends and Influence People* by Dale Carnegie, which I've done eight times. Good book. But Klassy's one technique incorporated almost every principle in Carnegie's book in one simple mental maneuver.

Here's what she does: She imagines walking around behind me and unzipping my back. She climbs inside and looks out my eyes, sees what I see, hears what I hear and hears it *the way* I hear it—from *my* point of view. She tries to imagine what it would feel like inside me. It's a very effective technique for *how* to walk a mile in someone's moccasins.

All my life I've heard the good advice: "Try to see things from the other person's point of view," but I always thought of it as metaphorical. Apparently it's *not* a figure of speech. It's a direct and perfectly clear instruction to *literally* imagine myself looking out through another's eyes. Their eyes *are* the points from which they view—not metaphorically, but in fact.

When I do this, it changes the way I feel about the person I'm listening to *and they can tell*. I don't know how, but people can tell I really understand them and that I'm not merely going through the motions of trying to *appear* as if I understand. And all I'm doing is seeing things from the other person's point of view—literally.

**Imagine yourself looking out
from inside another's body.**

Take the Sting Out

CRITICISM HURTS. So any decent person tries to avoid criticizing others. But sometimes you can't avoid it forever, so finally, when you get mad enough, you speak. The problem is, when you criticize while you're mad, you aren't likely to do it well. You'll say what the person did wrong instead of saying what you want him or her to do differently in the future. And when you say something while you're angry, the listener gets defensive because anger is an attacking emotion.

One way of getting around this is to *speak sooner*. Criticize *before* you get angry. Criticize when it first occurs to you and you won't have to "try to control yourself."

When you say it sooner, you'll naturally have more control over yourself. And people won't get very defensive because you're not attacking them. Oh, they might not like it. Nobody really *likes* being criticized. We would all prefer everyone loved us and showered us with gifts for just being ourselves. But that's not the way the world works. Criticism is a necessary part of relationships of any kind. Look at what happens to someone who never gets criticized. There have been people who have had so much power and money that everyone was afraid to criticize them: Hitler. Stalin. Sadaam Hussein. Howard Hughes. It made them lose touch with reality. You and I need criticism even though we don't like it.

And we need to criticize people. Not all the time, and it needs to be balanced with acknowledgments, but you can't go around *only* complimenting people—it isn't good for the people you work with or who live with you. You *must* criticize.

But say it early. Minimize the pain by not procrastinating. You'll say it better, the person will hear it better, you'll cause less pain and have more of an impact—the kind of impact you want to have on people: considerate and constructive.

And here is a tip on making a good criticism: Don't say what you didn't like; say what you would like in the future. Turn your complaint into a request. It is much easier to hear. For example, which would you rather hear: "You never pick up around here" or "Would you please pick up around here more often?" In other words, don't make them wrong for what they've done; just tell them what you want next time.

Speak up sooner and when you do, make requests. The end result is you'll get more of what you want from people, and they (and you) will be happier.

Criticize when it first occurs to you, and ask for what you want.

Honest criticism is hard to take, particularly from a relative, a friend, an acquaintance, or a stranger.

— *Franklin P. Jones*

Expressing anger and disagreement— airing a complaint—though rarely pleasant, makes the marriage stronger in the long run than suppressing the complaint.

— *John Gottman*

How to Be Close to Your Friends

IF JOE AND PETE ARE FRIENDS, they must have something in common: they went to the same school, work in the same place, etc. There are lots of possible things to have in common, but there is one that really makes a difference—one factor which, if it is held in common by Joe and Pete, can make them *close* friends.

That factor is *purpose* (aim, intention). If Joe and Pete are both *strongly* interested in the same purpose, they can be close friends.

So in order to have a close friend, you have to know what your own strongest interest is. What fires you up with passion for the subject? What do you love to talk about? What do you love to read about? What do you love to do? What do you strongly *desire*? When you know the answers to these questions, and when the answers are not a big list of things, but one major one, you've found your purpose.

Now that you know what your main intention or interest is, you can look at your friends and see which one or ones share that interest. Then, to get closer, you simply make the friendship center around that interest. Do things together along the lines of that interest; learn things about it and share what you've learned with your friend; empower each other and encourage each other to persist along those lines when the going gets tough. Do this and if you're honest with your friend, you can have a very close, warm friendship...a lifetime friendship.

If you look at your friends and none of them share your purpose, join clubs and associations that specialize in your interest area. Go to classes and meetings that center around your interest. Your chances are pretty good that you'll find a friend who can become a close fried. And a close friend is the best thing in the world for your health and happiness.

**Find and cultivate a friendship that
centers around your strongest interest.**

How to Have More Life in Your Time

TELEVISION IS A GREAT DEVICE for creating a little diversion when you want to give your mind a break. It's one of the few things we can do that doesn't present any challenge whatsoever. The problem is, the people who design the programming and the commercials don't want you to just take a little break and get back to living. They want you to keep watching. And over the years, they've developed hundreds of effective techniques to keep us hooked, and they're getting better at it all the time.

Studies at the University of Chicago found that when people are engaged in an activity like reading, talking, or pursuing a hobby, they become happier. Research also shows that the longer a person sits in front of a TV, the more irritable and dissatisfied they become. TV is entertaining, but it presents no challenge. Our minds and bodies start going stir crazy without a challenge. That's bad enough, but on top of that, commercials are specifically designed to make you feel dissatisfied (so you will buy their product to satisfy your "need").

You've got better things to do. If you want to gain more freedom from your television, try one of these ideas:

1. For one month, only watch videos—no TV with its seductive and addictive programming.

2. Cancel your cable: You'll save money and you'll have fewer stations to entice you.

3. Unplug the TV for a week.

EVERYONE IN YOUR household may thrash about like an addict in withdrawal, but hold firm and you'll see something remarkable: more human interaction, more walks together at sunset, more pursuits of hobbies, more reading. These are all things that aren't as easy as TV, but are more satisfying and rejuvenating.

Wean yourself away from your TV. Make it merely a peripheral activity—something you do once in awhile. Try one of the ideas above to protect yourself from the carefully-designed-to-be-addictive programming. You'll be glad you did.

Watch TV only once in awhile.

How to Melt Hard Feelings

THE HUMAN BRAIN IS *NOT* a blank slate at birth. Some general programs have been "hardwired." For example, when you're hungry and you smell your favorite food, your mouth waters. Any person on the planet has the same reaction, but to different foods. For you it may be apple pie; for a person in another culture, it may be curried cockroaches.

The *trigger* for the reaction is not built in, only the reaction. The same is true for the built-in reaction that causes hard feelings.

I'm talking about the impulse to defend something you own, feel a part of, or identify with. Most people feel a part of their family, so if your child or spouse was being attacked, you would defend them. If you saw someone breaking into your car, you might try to defend your car because you *own* it.

This built-in reaction played an important role during our evolution. The problem with that reaction now is that we've evolved to use symbols, so the same built-in reaction is triggered to defend our ideas, our beliefs, and our self-images. We can now identify with an *idea* of who we are, and when someone attacks that, it triggers a defensive reaction.

That's the source of hard feelings. Mildred says something to Harry that implies he isn't very strong. Part of Harry's idea of himself is that he is a *man* and part of his idea of manliness is that men are *strong*. So Mildred, perhaps without meaning to, has attacked something Harry has identified with, and whether Harry likes it or not, he will feel emotions appropriate to defending his home against intruders! In defense, he may attack something Mildred identifies with, and they now have hard feelings between them.

How can this kind of thing be avoided?

One thing that *doesn't* work is to say, "You're just being defensive." Most people's self-image includes, "I'm not a defensive person." So when you tell someone she's being defensive, you've just aroused that built-in reaction again!

A good rule of thumb is: Don't *tell* someone you aren't attacking, *demonstrate* you aren't attacking. Let people save face, give them the benefit of the doubt, point out your places of agreement, show respect for the other person's opinions, etc.

Do these sound familiar? Of course. They are common-sense ways of dealing with people, and you've probably used most of them many times. They are time-tested methods of handling those built-in defensive reactions in other people.

The problem is that you have the built-in mechanism in *yourself*. If you innocently step on someone's precious pride and he attacks you in an effort to defend himself, what happens? Before you can say "Boo," *your* built-in mechanism has been triggered. From that point it's pretty easy to slip into a downward spiral of hard feelings.

Here's the way out: When you notice yourself feeling defensive, *start talking to yourself* about the ideas in this chapter. Say to yourself, "I feel defensive, but the feeling is only from my *ideas*—nothing is threatening my family or my car or my body." Then *take the actions* of listening to and sympathizing with the other person's point of view. You can *act* undefensive even when you *feel* defensive, just as you can restrain yourself from hitting someone when you're mad. And when you do, you stop the downward spiral from going any further. You can do the intelligent thing even when you don't feel like it. And your intelligent actions will melt hard feelings like a spring thaw.

Act undefensive when you feel defensive.

How to Get What You Want From Others

PEOPLE LOVE TO BE APPRECIATED and they hate being told they're wrong. Given that, a good way to get what you want from others is to: 1) appreciate what you like, 2) ignore what you don't like, and 3) never indicate—even in your tone of voice or body language—you think they're wrong.

Let's look at the first part: Appreciate what you like. *Strongly appreciate* anything the person does that's *in the direction* of what you want. Tell her or him *why* you appreciate it, how much you enjoy it, how it makes you feel, and how, specifically, it makes your life easier, happier, or whatever. Detail works better than vagueness or generalities.

It works to let people know what you want from them *if* you can tell them without making them feel wrong. But once they know what you want, find every opportunity you possibly can—when they do what you want—to praise it! If you want him to pick up his clothes, and he picks up one sock, praise it! Forget the stuff he didn't pick up. Keep at this and you'll see more and more of what you want and less and less of what you don't want. Be specific: What exactly do you appreciate? Why specifically do you appreciate it? Don't expect quick results. Just be consistent and enthusiastic with your appreciation and avoid any attempt to make him feel wrong, and you'll see a gradual shift over to what you want.

When you do this, at first you may feel somewhat awkward or uncomfortable. Most of us aren't accustomed to giving sincere, heartfelt appreciation face to face. Keep at it. Push through it. You'll find the awkwardness fades and you'll also finds the rewards well worth your trouble.

Now about the second and third parts (they go together): Ignore what you don't like, and avoid making people feel wrong. If you make someone feel wrong, what will he do? Answer: Try to be right! He will make an excuse for it, he will try to justify it. He'll want to make himself feel right, *not change his ways*. If you give someone the opportunity to feel appreciated for what he does that you like, and if you also leave the rest alone, he is very likely to change his ways. But if you make him wrong, you actually make it harder for him to change.

The best way to get people to do what you want is to pretty much overlook what you *don't* want and enthusiastically appreciate what you *do* want. It's magic.

Downplay or overlook what you *don't* want and enthusiastically appreciate what you *do* want.

I can take any amount of criticism,
so long as it is unqualified praise.

— *Noël Coward*

Yes, you...possess powers...which you
habitually fail to use; and one of
those powers you are probably not using
to the fullest extent is your magic ability
to praise people and inspire them with
a realization of their latent abilities...
Abilities wither under criticism;
they blossom under encouragement.

— *Dale Carnegie*

Elicit Your Own Acknowledgment

EVERYONE NEEDS ACKNOWLEDGMENT. Not that we'll die without it, but it really makes a difference when we know other people know how good a job we're doing.

But not one in ten of us gets enough appreciation. A common reaction to this fact is that bosses and spouses should pay more attention; they should notice and then appreciate us. The problem is, *it is hard to notice the absence of a negative condition*. When you don't create problems and do your work well, and you allow other people to do their jobs unhindered, what is there to notice? Your good job becomes business as usual.

The juxtaposition of those two facts—everyone needs acknowledgment and it is hard to notice the absence of a negative condition—presents us with but one solution: You must *elicit* your own acknowledgment. You must point out your efforts to others when they don't notice.

But you can't do that! It's called bragging. And we've all met obnoxious, self-centered, boorish people who had a habit of talking about themselves and what they've accomplished. Bragging is offensive. Isn't it?

Yes it is—when it is done by obnoxious, self-centered people. When it is done by someone who simply wants to do a good job and stay motivated, eliciting acknowledgment can be a positive thing for everyone involved.

It might go something like this: You've been particularly careful about doing a certain thing, and you have been doing it consistently. *You* know this thing you're doing really helps out. *You* know things are working a lot better because you're putting in the time and effort to do this thing well. But since it helps everything go well, and since it is so difficult to notice an absence of a negative condition, no one notices you're doing such a good job. So when your spouse or boss is nearby, say to them, "I've been working very hard to make sure this thing goes right, and it's been going right. I just wanted someone to know."

Since we are all in the same boat, the person you're talking to will understand the feeling of simply wanting someone else to know, and you might even open up the possibility for him or her to do the same thing (elicit acknowledgment).

You don't have to force anything. You don't have to brag and swagger and say it over and over all the time until you brighten up the room every time you leave. You don't need to come from *deficiency*. You aren't *desperate* for attention. You're just helping yourself feel a little better about your work (and motivating yourself to keep it up) by letting someone know what you're doing.

Don't expect a lot. Some people will think it's strange that you pointed out your own good work. Some people will think you're bragging. Keep paying attention to the kinds of responses you get and keep modifying what you're doing until it is a simple acknowledgment of the facts. Also, get people to talk about what *they* are doing that they want someone to know about and then give them some acknowledgment for it. They will not only become more willing to acknowledge you for your accomplishments, but they will also be less likely to feel jealous when you point out something you did.

Elicit your own acknowledgment. It's better than grumbling that no one notices. It's not anyone's fault that no one notices. Because of the way our bodies, brains and the universe is constructed, it is just that way. Not much we can do about it but *use* it. You can bemoan the fact that gravity keeps you pinned to the Earth or you can accept it and get so good at dealing with it you can dance!

**When you want acknowledgment
for something, tell someone what you did.**

Self-Confidence

THE OPPOSITE OF SELF-CONFIDENCE is self-*consciousness*. To achieve self-confidence, then, all you need to do is get rid of your self-consciousness. But how? How do we get our attention off ourselves? Easy—by putting it somewhere else. And the easiest way to have your attention on something else is to *have a purpose of some kind.*

Let's see how this works. Let's say you're at a party and you're feeling self-conscious. The first question to ask is "Do you have some purpose for being at the party in the first place?" If you don't, a quick and easy way to stop feeling self-conscious would be to *leave the party.* But let's say you *do* have a purpose for being there.

Ask yourself, "What's my purpose here?" In other words, *what do you want?* What are you trying to accomplish? What are you after? Take a few moments and think about it. Would you like to make business contacts? Do you want to entertain people? Do you need information from somebody? Do you want to help bring people together? Do you want to meet someone? The question is: What is your aim or intention? If you don't have any purpose for being there, either go somewhere where you *do* have a purpose or make up some purpose. For example, during the course of the evening your purpose could be to find someone who knows where you can get a good math tutor for your child.

In a place I used to work, we had stretches of time with nothing to do, yet we had to be there. It left me with no purpose. So I made up purposes or made the situation serve other purposes of mine. Some of the employees spoke more Spanish than English, and I wanted to learn Spanish, so in the dead times, I'd teach them English and they'd teach me Spanish. Other times I needed new ideas for a project I was working on at home, and I asked my coworkers to help me, which they were glad to do.

Accomplish a goal. Make up a goal if you have to. Do you want to get rid of your self-consciousness? Put your attention on an aim. To have self-confidence, have a purpose. It's that simple.

**Relieve self-consciousness
by focusing on a purpose.**

The Power of a Poker Face

RONALD RIGGIO, PHD, has been doing research at the California State University at Fullerton for over seventeen years. He's been trying to find out what makes a person attractive to other people. He officially studies *charisma*. One important factor Riggio has discovered is the importance of "emotional expressivity": the ability to show your emotions on your face so people can easily read how you feel. People who don't show much emotion on their faces don't attract us very much. That's one of his findings that seems pretty obvious.

But Riggio found something that's not so obvious: Charisma also requires the ability to *not* show emotions.

He calls it "emotional control." It's what I'm calling a "poker face" because when you play poker and you get an exceptionally good hand, you don't want anyone else to know. Likewise, if you get a poor hand, you don't want them to know—it gives your opponents an advantage in betting against you. While you're playing poker, the basic rule of thumb is to not ever register your feelings overtly. The only thing that might give you away is the look on your face, so you have to show as little emotion on your face as you can.

Improving your ability to have a poker face *when you need it* (and only when you need it) can increase your effectiveness with people. Why? Because emotions are contagious *when they can be seen*. When you look at someone who is laughing, it tends to make you feel like laughing, doesn't it? Sure. And when you see someone crying, it can make you feel a little sad. Naturally. That's why good actors are so highly valued. They can make us feel emotions. We all have a tendency to experience the emotion we see on someone's face.

But, you may ask, what's wrong with that?

Nothing really, except sometimes. The problem is that there are some emotions you wouldn't want another to have. Two examples are anger and social awkwardness. When you're angry and you show it, the other person will probably become angry or defensive or afraid to some degree—they can see on your face your blood pressure is up, and their body will respond by increasing their own blood pressure. This rising intensity tends to interfere with communication.

Something similar happens when a person feels socially awkward. When you talk with someone who feels awkward because they don't quite know what to do *and it shows*, you feel somewhat awkward, too, don't you? Or how about when someone giving a speech feels uncomfortable up there in front of the group? Don't you also squirm in your seat a little just watching?

In these kinds of circumstances, the people would be better off and the people they're talking to would be better off if they would learn to conceal those particular emotions when they feel them.

We have all learned there are times when it is not appropriate to *say* certain things. You don't say to a widow at the funeral "the dude owed me money." At certain times and for certain situations, we all know some things are better left unsaid. Well, the emotion on your face is non-verbal, but it is still *communication*, and sometimes it is counterproductive to say nonverbally "I'm angry" or "I feel awkward."

The good news is that you can *learn* to put on a poker face when you need it. I'm not suggesting phoniness or pretending you're happy when you're angry. But there are times it helps to show *no* emotion on your face. It's a skill like any other, and it can be improved with practice.

**Practice having a "poker face"
when you feel negative emotions.**

TRUE Love

THERE ARE BASICALLY TWO WAYS TO TALK to your loved ones. The first is to hide some of your true wants and feelings, either by not expressing them at all or by being so indirect and "nice" that your loved ones don't know for sure how you really feel.

The other way is to be honest about what you want and feel.

The *results* of these two approaches are drastically different.

When you hide what you really want and feel, guess what? You *still* want and feel those things. Remember that point; it is important. You're afraid to say what you really want and feel because you think you'll be rejected, disapproved of, or disliked. The love might be withdrawn. Saying what you want or feel might start a fight or hurt someone's feelings.

Even though you have all these perfectly good and valid reasons to refrain from speaking up, that doesn't alter the fact that you *still* feel what you really feel and want what you actually want.

And those wants and feelings will come out, one way or another. Consciously or unconsciously, you'll try to manipulate the other person into doing what you want and your feelings will be expressed, no matter how hard you try to hide them. There are many ways. You can hint, tease, argue about it indirectly, try to make the other person feel guilty for not doing something, "accidentally" make mistakes, and so on. Not to mention that your body language and the subtle expressions on your face give you away. Your wants and feelings come out, even against your will.

The problem with these indirect, nonverbal, and often unconscious ways of communicating your feelings and wants is that *they are confusing*. And the confusion causes problems in close relationships.

It is difficult to be honest, and it can sometimes cause an upset. But honesty is not *confusing*. When you are saying what you really want and feel, problems can be worked out and solved. You can't solve a problem when you don't know what it's about.

So that's the choice: Withhold the truth or say it.

Of course, very few people are on either extreme. Every one of us hides our intentions and feelings from our loved-ones now and then, and at other times we're pretty frank. But any effort we make to move ourselves further toward the honest end of the spectrum will improve the quality of our close relationships over time.

If you want to be intimate, speak freely and honestly.

We think that white lies are socially acceptable, yet we bemoan the fact that our relationships are superficial.

— *M. Scott Peck*

The inferior man...attempts a hundred intrigues in order to save himself, but finishes only in creating a great calamity from which he cannot run away.

— *Wang Yang-Ming*

You water love with honesty.

— *J. Klassy Evans*

Too Polite?

YOU WERE TRAINED FROM DAY ONE to be polite and attentive to the wishes of others because, of course, it is the courteous thing to do. And when you're courteous, people won't be upset with you as often and you'll avoid uncomfortable confrontations and awkward moments.

It's perfectly understandable that parents would want their child to be polite. Parents don't like to be embarrassed. Besides, they want to help the child avoid being shunned by their peers. Being rude makes enemies. So does being selfish.

So it *is* important for parents to train their children to be courteous.

But there is also such a thing as "too much of a good thing." Courtesy and kindness can be *overlearned*—to the point where the person doesn't even *know* what he wants any more—where he'll stand there and listen to the worthless ramblings of an idiot who just likes to talk, without the guts to be "rude" and excuse himself because he's got better things to do.

Someone who has overlearned politeness will be too easily persuaded by family members that such-and-such is right and good, only to figure out later that it's *not* right and good for *him*, now that he thinks about it.

When you don't know what you want—when politeness dominates self-awareness—*other* people's wants hold the floor for lack of opposition. They win by default, as when two parties are scheduled for a hearing and one of the parties doesn't show. The one who shows up wins automatically by default.

What's lacking when you're too polite is a healthy level of selfishness. If you've been trained from early on to suppress your own wishes, you may suppress them right out of existence. And that doesn't benefit anybody.

This kind of unhealthy politeness only happens in relation to others. Just about everyone can pursue their own agenda when they're by themselves. It is *in the presence of other people* that the social inhibitions laid down in childhood exert their powerful influence. What they influence are our *feelings*.

What's missing is a simple knowledge of what we want, what we ourselves would like to see happen, and the willingness to try to make it happen—even when someone else might not like it. And what's needed is the willingness to *say* what we want.

If you are suffering from excess courtesy, here's what to do: Start small. In little situations every day, make small goals. Ask yourself "What do I want here?" or "What do I think would be the best thing to happen in this situation?" And then try to make it happen.

Inevitably, you'll run into someone else with a different agenda. This other person has a different outcome in mind. She doesn't know about your goal. So you need to let her know what you want.

Sometimes you'll feel like you're being rude. Sometimes the other person will *think* you're rude. If, like you, she's been overtrained in courtesy and undertrained in healthy selfishness, she'll take up your agenda and help make it happen, or at least she won't oppose you.

If, on the other hand, she *is* able to say what she wants, the two of you can negotiate. One way or the other, you need to know what you want and you must be willing to speak up about it.

Know what you want and speak up about it.

---

*You can't be afraid of stepping on toes
if you want to go dancing.*

— *Lewis Freedman*

Right Makes Might

ONCE YOU'VE MADE UP YOUR MIND about something, your mind works overtime to make itself right. Tell yourself "I have a high energy level" and your mind will try to make you right about that—you'll find energy reserves you didn't know you had, or your mind will fool you and make you *think* and *feel* you have more energy than you "really" do. Either way is better than feeling tired.

The same forces operate just as effectively with something negative. Say to yourself "I just don't seem to have the energy I had when I was younger" and your mind will make you right. Even if it's not true, the times you feel tired will stand out in your memory, and moments of high energy will be disqualified, dismissed, or forgotten.

Change what you say to yourself about people you don't get along with and your mind will work overtime to make yourself right. If you say she's a jerk, *your* actions will tend to bring out her jerkiness when she's around you *because you want to be right*. If you say to yourself she just had a bad day or is improving every day, your actions will subtly influence her behavior in a way that makes you right. You have the power. It's not absolute and almighty, but what you say to yourself influences your state of mind, the way you treat others, and thus the way they treat you.

Since you have a mind that tries to be right, you might as well use it. Make sure the things you say to yourself about yourself and other people are things you want to be right about. And you will be.

Say things to yourself you want to be right about.

Let us have faith that right makes might;
and in that faith let us, to the end,
dare to do our duty as we understand it.

— *Abraham Lincoln*

The Bad Apples

WHEN DALE CARNEGIE wrote his classic book on human relations, *How to Win Friends and Influence People,* he left out a chapter; it wasn't finished on time, so the book was published without it. The chapter was supposed to cover the subject of dealing with people you *cannot* win with.

For most people, when you treat them fairly, they treat you fairly in return. But as you know, there exists in this world a small percentage of people who will simply take advantage of you when you try to treat them fairly. There are people who will play games with you, deceive you, and some who will actively prevent you from making your relationship work. Carnegie's unwritten chapter was for the times when "somebody has to go to jail, be spanked, divorced, knocked down, sued in court."

Even beyond those extreme cases, every once in awhile you'll get stuck working with or having to interact with someone who continually brings you down or in some way makes your life difficult. They may *seem* to be very nice people. They might smile and come across with a lot of charm. But the end result of your interactions are: You're worse off. You try to make things work, you try to be fair, and you get the short end of the stick every time. You've tried to talk with them, perhaps, and it doesn't make things better, and they probably make you feel bad for saying anything.

I have no fancy methods for dealing with these people. You can't really deal with them. If they're doing something illegal, you can certainly call the police, but most are too clever to do something illegal. My wife uses a good analogy in her speeches. She says trying to make things work with these people is like trying to wrestle with someone who is covered with mud: You're going to get muddy. No matter what you do or how well you do it or how noble your intentions, you'll get muddy.

So instead of trying to make things work out with these people, the goal is to avoid dealing with them at all. Go for *minimal impact*. Have as little to do with them as you can get away with (without causing yourself trouble). Ideally, you would eliminate them from your life completely. Stop calling, stop visiting, stop being nice. You don't have to be mean about it. Just fade them into the background and then all the way out of the picture.

I know this isn't a perfect world. Sometimes you'll have to keep interacting with someone who won't let you make things work. So go as far as you can to minimize their effect on your life. Talk to them as little as you can, look at them as little as you can. Focus your attention on your purpose and on the rest of the people around you.

When you come across someone and nothing works with him, cut your losses. Don't waste any more effort trying. This is a big world full of wonderful people and a few bad apples. Concentrate your attention on the good people and waste as little of your attention as you can on the ones who bring you down. You can do it a little at a time and it will improve your attitude. And if it improves your attitude, it's good for your relationships with your family and friends, and it's good for your health.

Try not to waste too much of your attention on people who bother you.

---

*Expecting the world to treat you fairly
because you are a good person is a little
like expecting a bull not to attack you
because you're a vegetarian.*

— Quoted by Dennis Wholey

Refuse to Flinch

EVERYBODY KNOWS what it means to flinch. Example: You pretend you're going to slug me, and I twitch or blink. I flinched. Now let's expand and extend that idea in a useful way: Let's say flinching is *any* form of shrinking back, pulling away or turning aside, *when it's done to avoid discomfort or difficulty*.

Have you ever noticed that you have a strong desire to put your hands in front of your body when you're standing up and talking to several people who are all seated? Most people do. If you *succumb* to your desire to put your hands in front of your body, that's a flinch.

Or say you're telling someone something she doesn't want to hear. While you talk, maybe you shift your body's weight from one foot to another, pick at your fingernails or cross your arms. You flinched!

If you look at someone and they then look at you and you quickly look away, you flinched. Mumbling or speaking quietly is a form of flinching. Someone who is avoiding going to night classes because he's afraid he might not do well is flinching.

Flinching is an attempt to protect yourself, and it's very natural. Everybody does it. But there is one major problem with it: Flinching makes you weak. Notice I didn't say it was a sign that you are weak. The act of flinching *itself* makes you weak.

But when you have the urge to flinch and you don't, you gain a kind of strength. And when you look people right in the eyes with your arms hanging by your sides where they naturally hang and you speak truthfully without flinching, you have an unnervingly powerful personal presence.

And you don't have to spend years getting good at this; you can do it the very next time you talk to someone. It's easy to do (once you decide to), but when you do it, you will notice a temptation, a craving, a desire—almost an ache—to fidget or look away or at least put your hands in your pockets.

Refuse to flinch.

Make up your mind—as soon as you notice yourself flinching—that you will not flinch. You'll like the result. A fear just goes out of you. This is especially true if you consider yourself shy to any degree. Don't flinch, and suddenly the sense of shyness becomes somewhat wispy and transparent, and you'll start to wonder if there has ever been anything there but a shadow.

Don't flinch, and feel the power.

Then go on and expand this power by extending the practice into the psychological arena. When someone is "in denial," it means they are mentally or emotionally flinching; they are looking away or shrinking back or avoiding something real—some truth, some reality—and always *in order to avoid discomfort or difficulty.*

But always and forever, wherever you flinch, you will be weak. And wherever you refuse to flinch, you will be strong.

This is the "how" of courage. It's not that during a courageous act a person doesn't *want* to run away. What makes it courageous is that the person wants to run away *but doesn't.* Courage is refusing to flinch.

Extend your unflinching psyche into any area where you want more personal power.

If you want to be socially strong, don't flinch in social situations. If you want to be emotionally strong, don't flinch at emotional feelings or situations. You would benefit if you made this a lifetime practice, a spiritual regimen, a holy discipline.

Wherever you refuse to flinch, you will have power. This will, of course, increase your impact on people. People will admire your courage and look up to you. When this happens, don't flinch.

Resist the temptation to flinch.

Forging Mettle

METTLE IS A WORD you don't hear much these days. It means a strength of mind that gives you the ability to withstand pain or difficulties with bravery and resolution. Mettle is a quality we all admire. But it isn't something you are born with. It must be *developed*. It is strengthened by the way you conduct your everyday life. Specifically, mettle is created by daily making the decision to:

> **Remain loyal to your comrades.** We are social creatures, and when you violate this cannon, you wound yourself at the core. If you are married and find yourself flirting with someone at work,

make the decision to remain loyal to your spouse, even if it means not getting the admiring eyes of another. If someone is bad-mouthing a friend of yours behind their back, defend them in their absence. When you have committed yourself to someone, whoever they are, remain true to them. This is one of the deepest principles of integrity.

Speak honestly and directly. We live in a world of appearances and game-playing. It is one of the things that makes the world a crazy place and produces so much stress. More honesty in the world is needed and wanted, from the smallest level all the way up. Honesty requires courage, and it exacts a price. And although you will never be *perfectly* honest, you can always improve. It is the effort to increase your integrity that forges mettle.

Keep your word. Be careful about what you promise or what promises you imply. Be very clear with others about what they can expect from you and clear and careful with yourself about what you can expect from yourself. And then do everything you can to never disappoint. Keep your word. Think of your word as sacred and treat it so. It produces one of the finest experiences known to humankind: trust. People will learn they can count on you, and *you* will learn you can count on yourself.

THESE ARE THE Three Commandments of Mettle. Courage may seem like an ancient and unneeded quality in our pampered modern era, but now we need it more than ever. The human race is controlling the destiny of all living things on earth, and what is needed is human integrity. The place to start is your own. The time to start is now. Give your spouse and children an example to emulate and you will be doing the most concrete good you can for the future of the planet.

To forge mettle:
Remain loyal to your comrades, speak honestly and directly, and keep your word.

There is only one way to cope with life, namely, to find that system of values which is not subject to fashionable trends...which will never change, and will always bear fruit in terms of bringing us peace and health and assurance...
— *Thomas Hora*

Be the change you want to see in the world.
— *Mohandas K. Gandhi*

People Principles

Relax your muscles and make it your mission to help the *other* person feel more comfortable.

To improve the self-esteem of others:
**Give unexaggerated feedback
and help them gain ability.**

To improve your own self-esteem:
**Change what you *do* to make yourself
more appreciated by the people around you.**

**Direct all complaints to the person
who can do something about it.**

Question and criticize your negative judgements of people.

As a personal discipline, practice listening well when someone is talking to you.

Increase your certainty about how to act.

Clean up relationships by being honest without judgement.

Try to make a good first impression.

Act like a person who is well liked and worthy of respect, even when you don't feel that way.

Don't say much when you're angry.

When you complain, say what you want, not what you don't want.

To find and keep a good mate:
Pursue your interest and remind yourself: Nobody's perfect and attraction to others is unimportant.

Encapsulate your insights into short phrases
and repeat them often.

Play yourself down.

Be honest. If it causes conflict, listen well
and only say what is strictly true.

Practice E-Squared now and then:
Pay close attention to your ongoing experience.

Notice how other people are similar to you.

Send good wishes to people anytime, anywhere.

Don't limit yourself by giving yourself
a narrow label.

Accept the natural conflict
between parent and child.

Set standards and enforce them
with consequences.

Influence people by merely suggesting things.

**When you talk to people,
think of them as relatives.**

**Improve children's self-esteem by
helping them become more competent.**

Be overly clear with people.

**Imagine yourself looking out
from inside another's body.**

**Criticize when it first occurs to you,
and ask for what you want.**

**Find and cultivate a friendship that
centers around your strongest interest.**

Watch TV only once in awhile.

Act undefensive when you feel defensive.

**Downplay or overlook what you *don't* want and
enthusiastically appreciate what you *do* want.**

When you want acknowledgment for something,
tell someone what you did.

Relieve self-consciousness
by focusing on a purpose.

Practice having a "poker face"
when you feel negative emotions.

If you want to be intimate,
speak freely and honestly.

Know what you want and speak up about it.

Say things to yourself you want to be right about.

Try not to waste too much of your attention
on people who bother you.

Resist the temptation to flinch.

To forge mettle:
Remain loyal to your comrades, speak honestly
and directly, and keep your word.

Parting Shot

YOU NOW HAVE IN YOUR POSSESSION 117 tested, proven principles. Apply them and they will work for you. But watch out for two sneaky, tricky factors that can spoil your progress: enthusiasm and greed.

Enthusiasm is a powerful force, and, like electricity or nuclear power, it is important to control that power carefully or it can fry you. Too much enthusiasm can cause overwhelm and burnout.

Greed isn't too far from enthusiasm. Remember the children's story of the goose that laid the golden eggs? Its lesson applies to this book. The owner of the goose didn't want to wait for the golden eggs to come out one at a time. He killed the goose to get all the eggs right away and he wound up with nothing. If you try to get all the value contained within these pages *quickly*, if you try to apply too many principles at once, you will reap very little constructive change. Most changes require concentration and it is a limitation of the human mind that it cannot concentrate on many things at once.

Choose a few, preferably only *one* principle, and *concentrate on it.* Make it your theme for a few days, a week, a month. At some point you will have gained a certain naturalness or automaticity with it—a mastery—and it will then be time to choose another principle to concentrate on.

Although this seems a slow way, it's the best way to reap the most benefits in the long run. I wish you well.

Concentrate on only one principle at a time.

Anything worth doing is worth doing now.

— J. Klassy Evans

May you live all the days of your life.

—Jonathan Swift

Contact Points

I hope you enjoyed this book and will continue to enjoy it in the future. I would love to hear from you for any reason. Write to me at this address:

Adam Khan
c/o YouMe Works
PO Box 1703
Bellevue, WA 98009

or e-mail me:

AdamKhan@aol.com

Visit our web site:

www.YouMeWorks.com

Index